L. M. P.

Lidia Donati

A Tale of Florence

L. M. P.

Lidia Donati
A Tale of Florence

ISBN/EAN: 9783742800190

Manufactured in Europe, USA, Canada, Australia, Japa

Cover: Foto ©Andreas Hilbeck / pixelio.de

Manufactured and distributed by brebook publishing software (www.brebook.com)

L. M. P.

Lidia Donati

'It was a Fiesole Villa.'

Frontispiece.

A TALE OF FLORENCE.

BY

L. M. P.

R WASHBOURNE,

To

MY DEAREST ITALIAN FRIEND,

G****** C********* C*********.

LIDIA DONATI.

CHAPTER I.

It was a Fiesole villa.

Above stretched the cloudless blue sky of Italy; below in the valley, at the foot of the Fiesole hill, lay Florence basking in the sunshine among hills covered with vineyards and olive-groves.

On the other side of the tall and stately towers that rise out of the city, the olive-trees on the hills were shining gray in the sunlight. The old church of San Miniato crowned the height of Monte alle Croci, and rose clear against the soft Italian sky, and the gold mosaic over the church door was glittering in the brilliant sun. Outside the city of Florence the Arno wound its way like a silver serpent in and out of the vineyards of

Tuscany. The blue Lucchese mountains, the white Carrara hills beyond them, shut in the rich Valley of the Arno; over it all hung a faint rose-coloured mist, the charm of Italian landscapes. It was a peaceful scene. No sound or bustle of the town reached this Fiesole villa on the side of the luxuriant hill. A dark cypress avenue led up to it from the white zigzag road. The walls of the house were decorated with many quaint designs after the fashion of all the old villas round Florence, built in the time when the city ranked among the most powerful in the world.

There was a broad terrace facing the drawing-room windows, and a shady *loggia* on the roof.

A lady and gentleman stood on the terrace of the Villa Donati. The sun shining on the landscape round fell on the aristocratic features and stately figure of the Marchesa Donati and her companion, a man of some five or six and thirty years of age, with a thoughtful brow and a grave kindness in his eyes that lent a charm to a face which could not otherwise be called handsome.

They had been silent for many moments, but at length the Marchesa Donati turned slowly to her companion, bitter humiliation written on her proud face.

'Then we are ruined?' she said.

'No, not quite,' answered the gentleman. 'You forget the race has not been lost, Marchesa. Who knows but——'

She interrupted him with an impatient gesture.

'If it is lost, what will happen? Marchese Vanutelli, do not fear to tell me the truth.'

'If all is lost Carlo will have to work,' answered her companion gravely; 'but let us hope such a possibility will not occur. Should it be so, you may still be able in course of time to recover everything.'

The quiet face was earnest and quivering with emotion. The Marchesa was touched.

'Thank you for your sympathy, kind friend,' she said, 'and for your goodness in telling me what my son should have told me himself. I cannot thank you enough for the kind part you have taken in this unhappy affair, neither can I understand the boy's cowardice.'

The Marchesa's voice was steady, and her face calm and impressive; only the tight, convulsive clasp of the white hands betrayed her deep emotion.

'Do not look at it in that light,' said her companion. He knew well enough the mother's words were true, but, with his usual kindness, he tried to alleviate the pain she was feeling. 'It would be quite natural for Carlo to be grieved and ashamed of what he has done. He finds it hard to face his mother, to——'

'You are wrong,' she interrupted; 'a son who was truly grieved for having brought ruin on his mother would have come immediately and asked her pardon. It is true, words to express his sorrow might fail him; but he would have faced the humiliation of confession bravely as his punishment—not deputed a friend to tell the bitter story to his mother. Do not tell me, Marchese, you would have acted as Carlo has done.'

'We are made very differently one from another,' he said; 'we cannot judge others by ourselves.'

The Marchesa Donati looked at him in silence; she shook her head, then began walking slowly backwards and forwards on the terrace.

'This will be my death-blow,' she continued, confronting him; and, indeed, the last few minutes had seemed to bring out the hard lines on her face. 'Not even your kindness, Marchese, in breaking this news to me has been able to lessen the blow of my son's cowardice. Not a word! It *is* cowardice; I prefer to call it by its proper name, not smooth it over by a prettier word. When I go, Lidia will be confided to her brother's care. I cannot leave her to anyone else, for we are the only Donatis. My niece Giulia Mirandoli is not over-rich to be burdened with a penniless cousin. Should I be called away before I see you again, you will look after her: is it not so? You will see that she is happy—that her brother does not oppress her with his selfishness. She will soon be leaving the convent where she has been educated to return home. In asking you to look after her, I feel I could not confide the trust to worthier hands.'

The Marchesa held out her hand to her companion as she finished speaking.

'You are agitated,' he said gravely, 'by this news. There is no need for me to promise to comply with your wishes, thank God! You have still your health and strength, Marchesa, which I trust will bring you to a happy old age.'

The Italian lady smiled sadly.

'Ah! old age has come already,' she answered; 'twenty years have been added to my life this day. It will please me if you will consent to my—let us call it whim, if you like, even though you may not think it necessary.'

Marchese Vanutelli bent and kissed her hand.

'I do promise to look after the child,' he said fervently, 'should—which God forbid—the occasion require it. My first thought will be to see to her welfare and happiness, as her mother would have wished, and before that thought all others shall give way.'

The Marchese spoke with an earnestness he seldom showed, and as she looked up at the face before her, the Marchesa knew he would be true to his word.

'Thank you,' she answered; 'I knew you

would never fail us. It grieves me to think you are leaving Florence——'

'Only for a short time,' he interrupted. 'I have some business to transact in Sicily. If you want me during the next week, do not hesitate to send for me. It grieves me much to leave you in your time of anxiety. Shall I send Carlo to you?'

'Ah, he is afraid to come!' exclaimed the Marchesa, with a bitter smile, which it would be difficult to see without pitying the woman who felt her son's conduct so keenly. The Marchese Vanutelli's face changed. True distress shone out of his quiet eyes on the poor mother; she saw it, and altered her voice, her face struggling to be calm. 'Yes; send him to me,' she said. 'Addio, and may God reward you!'

When her companion had left her, the Marchesa stood motionless by the parapet of the terrace. Though her eyes were turned towards the city below, she saw little of the fair scene before her. Bitter anger was filling her heart against the son who had so cruelly disappointed her. Her life had indeed assumed a different aspect since her husband's death, five years before. While he was alive she had lived in luxury, no wish ever denied her; but now all was changed. Her only son was a spendthrift, and had squandered away his fortune among the wild set of young men in Florence who think it manly to scoff at religion and all holy things. No sense of honour restrained him. Having lost all his own money, he never paused to scruple about helping himself to his mother's and sister's. Not that he actually took it from them, but his bills poured in, and had to be paid to save the family honour.

And now the crisis had come. Marchese Vanutelli, an old friend of the family, was the one chosen by Carlo to break the news to his mother. Perhaps Carlo knew the Marchese would endeavour to represent his conduct in a better light than was possible for himself to do. He knew she had always respected Marchese Vanutelli. Perhaps she might be reasoned with to look on their possible ruin in a less severe light than if her son had told her. But, unfortunately, the young man chose a line of conduct which only served to irritate his mother, who at once set it down to its true cause—cowardice. And that was the one thing the Marchesa Donati despised. The realization that it had proved to be the nature of her son was, as she had said, a death-blow to the proud Marchesa.

The extent of the expenditure of the last few years had not fully dawned upon her until the Marchese Vanutelli had opened her eyes by telling her of the race on which Carlo had staked their all. The latter had made the acquaintance of a wealthy Englishman in Rome the year before. Mr. Treherne was able to afford what his Italian friend could not, but the Marchese Donati did not understand this. He was annoyed the Englishman should be thought better off, and therefore be more sought after in Florence than he was ; and so this year Carlo had been spending lavishly, and had now staked his all—nay, more than his all—on the Roman race with Mr. Treherne. It was this he had been afraid to tell his mother, knowing it would rouse all the passionate Italian nature, before which Carlo had so often quailed. On the afternoon of the day on which he intended leaving for Sicily, the Marchese Vanutelli had gone up to the Fiesole villa, and Carlo had asked him to break the news to his mother.

It must be acknowledged that Carlo felt somewhat ashamed of himself, as the Marchese's quiet though reproachful words fell on his ears; they haunted him unpleasantly afterwards. 'He was his mother's only son, and she was a widow; it should have been his place to be the comfort of her days; on him she thought to lean with entire confidence now that his father was dead. How had he repaid the love and devotion his mother had shown him since his infancy?'

That a complete reconciliation should be effected between the mother and son seemed almost impossible, but the Marchese Vanutelli was not the man to declare anything impossible unless he had first tried to surmount the difficulty.

Alas! the Marchesa was bitterly humiliated. She stood now on the terrace, her hands clasped convulsively, waiting for her son.

Approaching footsteps told her he was

near. She turned round slowly, and confronted him. He was very dark and handsome, thus bearing a striking resemblance to the Marchesa; but there was a careless smile on his sarcastic mouth, as though he wished to hide any emotion he might feel.

For a full minute she gazed on him in silence, and when she spoke Carlo Donati knew he had misunderstood his mother's character, and that she would have taken their ruin much less to heart had he come to her himself and confessed everything.

'I have been told of this Roman race,' she said slowly, as though pausing to choose her words. 'So you deputed Marchese Vanutelli to make your confession for you? It was bravely—nobly done!'

She stood back from him, her dark eyes gaining life from the anger that flashed from them.

'Without a spark of pride or honour yourself,' she went on, hardly waiting to see the effect of her words, 'you did not think I should feel an outsider telling me of my son's disgrace. The Marchese Vanutelli acted as he has always done—with the kind courtesy befitting a gentlemen—and he did not fail in what must have been a hard task: telling a mother her son had ruined her.'

A dark frown gathered over the young man's face.

'Ruined!' he repeated; 'that is nonsense—pure exaggeration!'

'You think so,' said his mother bitterly. 'What I have asked you many times to do—is that also nonsense? When I told you that we were not rich, and when I tell you now that you—yes, you, Carlo—have spent all we have, that your friend the Englishman is wealthy, and can afford what we cannot—is that pure exaggeration?'

'I suppose you want me to give up the Roman race?' cried her son, flushing under the taunting words he knew were true; 'and I will not. Vanutelli had the same idea. I cannot draw back, and I shall win. Treherne has not the faintest chance, and he knows it.'

'He knows it!' repeated the Marchesa. 'Ah, what a disinterested man he must be! Merely for the pleasure of betting he stakes an immense sum with the certainty it will be lost. If you do not win,' she went on, 'you will lose not a little, nor the greater part, but everything!'

'I cannot lose everything!' exclaimed Carlo Donati impetuously, avoiding his mother's glance. 'Signor Treherne is my friend; this business is entirely between us two. If I lose, he can afford to wait, and perhaps help me a little.'

Hardened as he was, Carlo shrank from the gaze his mother fixed upon him. For a few moments she could not speak; her haughty face was white and quivering.

'So you would stoop so low?' she said, in a voice that seemed to pierce through the listener like a sharp knife. 'You have not scrupled to squander your sister's money and mine when you had lost your own. Now you have staked our all with this Englishman, whom, God knows, I thought an honourable man. Doubtless I was mistaken, for how could a man of honour associate with you?'

It was sad to hear the mother's voice, and see her stony gaze turned on her son.

'And now,' she went on, 'you would dishonour the name you bear! You have given me an insight into what will happen after my death. To benefit yourself, you would disgrace your name.'

The Marchesa Donati clasped her hands and bowed her head. A sullen scowl had spread over the young man's face, but he was silent.

'Hear me out now, Carlo,' said his mother, in a more subdued tone. 'This blow has been heavy indeed. God has seen fit to punish me through my son. This awakening has shortened my life by many years. When I go, Lidia will be given to your charge. As I told the Marchese Vanutelli, to no one else can I leave her, for I would not burden Giulia with an extra expense; but—and God hears me!—to no one could I leave her with less confidence than to her own brother. If you lose the race, the debt to this Englishman must and shall be paid. We will give him this villa and go and live at Quaracchi—if that also has not been sold. I will tell Lidia of my wishes in case I be not spared to see all arranged as I should wish.'

She paused for his answer. A hard, bitter expression settled round her mouth as she looked at her son standing sullen and defiant before her; but Carlo Donati gave no reply, and his mother walked slowly into the house, leaving him gazing over the valley below.

The Marchesa did not shut her eyes to the fact that if her son lost the race they would be ruined but for their house at Quaracchi, an old farm-house situated in the plain outside Florence, and surrounded by its vineyards and olive-groves. She knew they had not sufficient to pay the enormous sum staked; they had no relations to whom they could turn in their distress, only the Contessa Mirandoli, the late Marchese's niece; but she and her husband were by no means wealthy. At present they were in Switzerland endeavouring to live more economically than they could in Florence. The Contessa was a bright little lady of seven or eight and twenty, and had proved an exception to the rule of Italian girls. Out of sheer perverseness, her father declared, she fell in love with the poor Conte Mirandoli, and he, grave man of seven-and-thirty though he was, could not withstand the gay chattering little fairy. They gained the day at last, just six years ago, when her father, fairly tired out by her persevering entreaties, and determination to gain her point, consented to the marriage. The Conte Giulio Donati was now dead, having survived his elder brother by only a year, and his wife had died when Giulia was a baby.

It was useless to apply to them, and even had they been in easier circumstances, the Marchesa was too proud and independent a woman to be willing to be under obligations to anyone. Without hesitation, therefore, she decided that, should Carlo lose, her much-loved home at Fiesole should go towards paying the debt to the Englishman.

CHAPTER II.

The race on which the fortunes of the Donati family depended was over.

It was late at night. The moon was lighting up the hills and valleys, the vineyards and olive-groves, and the serpent-winding river. Florence, with its domes and towers, was sleeping peacefully below.

Carlo Donati walked slowly up the dark cypress avenue of his home.

He started back suddenly as a black figure seemed to rise out of the ground in front of him. It roused him from thoughts that were by no means pleasant ones. The peaceful air around had somehow only served to irritate him; he wondered how it was that some lives were full of adversities while others are filled with happiness.

'Carlo!' exclaimed a girlish voice, as the speaker caught hold of his arm.

'What are you wandering about here for at this time of night?' asked Carlo hoarsely, for he was considerably startled. 'What do you want?'

'I waited to meet you. Tell me what has happened!' she entreated, trying to read his face in the darkness.

'I have lost,' he answered abruptly. 'Well, Lidia, why do you stand there looking like a ghost?'

He shook her hand off his arm.

'Do not frighten mother,' she said, in a low voice, her pale face growing paler still. 'Let me go first and tell her.'

Carlo did not object. As before, he quailed in his heart before the meeting and the avowal. He left his sister standing under the swinging lamp in the lofty old-fashioned hall, with its rafter-ceiling.

Lidia Donati was at this time little more than a child, only just seventeen. A few days back she had left the convent where she had been brought up ever since she was five years old. There was little of her mother's haughty beauty in the sweet pale face, except that the small mouth was firm, and proudly her chief beauty—soft Italian eyes, with a steadfast light which made you turn to her instinctively for sympathy, and you would surely find it. She was of middle height, rather too thin to be called a good figure, but there was grace in her movements as she went towards her mother's room.

The Marchesa Donati was standing near the door when her daughter entered, her head bent forward as though she were listening.

'It was his step!' she exclaimed on seeing Lidia. 'Carlo has returned!'

'Yes,' replied her daughter gently; 'he is here. He will be with you soon, dear mother.'

'Oh, speak out!' cried the Marchesa, with quick instinct; 'do not fear to tell me the truth. He has lost. Dio mio!'

She paced the room quickly; all her passionate Italian nature was aroused.

'Lost all to this Englishman!' she continued, wringing her hands, 'who has already more than he knows what to do with. Lidia, why do you stand so still, looking at me with your great black eyes? Do something! do something!'

'We must think, mamma mia,' said Lidia.

'Think!' broke out her imperious mother sharply. 'It requires no thinking! All—all must go to this Englishman. Do you think I shall put myself under any obligation to him, as your brother would have me do? No! I would rather work. From the very first I knew Carlo would lose this mad race.'

'Oh, mamma, if I could only comfort you a little!' exclaimed Lidia; and, going up to her mother, she took her hand and caressed it. The Marchesa was silent, seeming as though she did not notice the quiet gesture; but after a few moments had elapsed she smoothed the brown head resting on her shoulder.

The door opened slowly and Carlo came in with a defiant air, though his face was paler than usual. Without a word he sank into the nearest chair.

His mother drew herself away from Lidia and looked at him, no love lingering in her cold dark eyes.

'And now,' she said bitterly, 'you had better go and buy the organ.'

'And the money?' asked her son mockingly. Perhaps Carlo Donati thought it more manly to pretend he did not care.

There was a pause; then the mother spoke:

'To-morrow you will go to the Signor Inglese and pay him all you can; the house will cover what you cannot give in money. There are many valuable things the signore may accept in lieu of payment——'

The Marchesa Donati's voice failed her. Perhaps she remembered how dear to her were all these things she was giving up.

'Do you think that no one has accepted an offer without demeaning himself before now?' burst forth Carlo—'that if Treherne were willing to come to an agreement my honour would be compromised?'

'You may live on the charity of this Englishman,' said his mother quietly, 'but I and your sister will go elsewhere. You may stay here on the bounty of your friend, spending his money, living under his roof, but Lidia and I will work. She has her painting, and perhaps I can find something to do. Is it not so, Lidia?'

Lidia bowed her head.

Carlo rose. He looked sullenly from his mother to his sister. He had been brought up knowing no will but his own. His father and mother had been foolishly indulgent to their only son, and things had turned out as they generally do in such cases. Carlo Donati seldom, if ever, thought of anyone but himself. The Marchesa, being a woman of deep feeling, where she did not reverence and love, hated and despised. Only she herself knew what a bitter disappointment her son's selfish, cowardly nature was to her, and she judged harshly, never pausing to think that much of it was her own doing. Her proud, passionate nature was stung to the quick by the indifference of the son she had well-nigh worshipped.

'You wish to be set down in the Martyrs' Calendar,' said Carlo roughly. 'Remember it——'

'Oh, Carlo!' entreated his sister, interrupting him, 'do not speak lightly of the Church and of holy things. It is God's Church. We were talking of things far removed from it.'

'It is easy for you,' cried Carlo angrily. 'You speak of working, but you know you will shirk it all in a convent, and live on the fat of the land, and I must go begging about, having no desire to put on a habit. It is good and holy to preach; those are the most eloquent who have the least to bear.'

'Do you think, then, that your sister has little to bear?' asked the Marchesa sternly. 'Look into her future! Is it full of riches and comfort, such as she ought to have, or poverty——'

'Mamma!' exclaimed Lidia, 'that does not matter; I——'

'Silence!' said the mother imperiously. 'You interrupt me!—Or poverty to which you have condemned her, so that she must work for her living?'

'There is no need for her to work for her living,' muttered Carlo.

'Silence!' repeated the Marchesa Donati. 'I marvel at your courage! How is it you can stand there defiant, as though you were the aggrieved one, when it is you who have turned us out of our home? Doubtless your nature is better fitted than your mother's for the world. You can endure the bitterest humiliations, listen to the sharpest taunts, without a sense of injured pride or honour. O Dio mio! You knew when you gave me a son who would be a disgrace to his name that no punishment could be greater, no torment more bitter!'

The Marchesa's arms fell powerless to her side. Her daughter came softly up to her, and kissed her white face. It seemed to rouse her mother.

'We will retire now,' she said. 'Carlo,' and she turned to her son, 'I have said hard and bitter things to you, for which I repent; I pity you, my son, with all my heart. Your nature is your punishment, and it is not for me to condemn.—Lidia, you will come with me; I wish to speak to you for awhile.'

She waited for an answer, but her son's face was turned away; he would not look at his mother.

'Good-night,' she said, laying her hand on his shoulder. 'Good-night, my son!'

But still no answer came, so she held out her hand to Lidia, and they left the room together.

'We will arrange what we can to-morrow,' she said to her daughter.

But, alas! there was no to-morrow for the Marchesa Donati. Her own words, that she

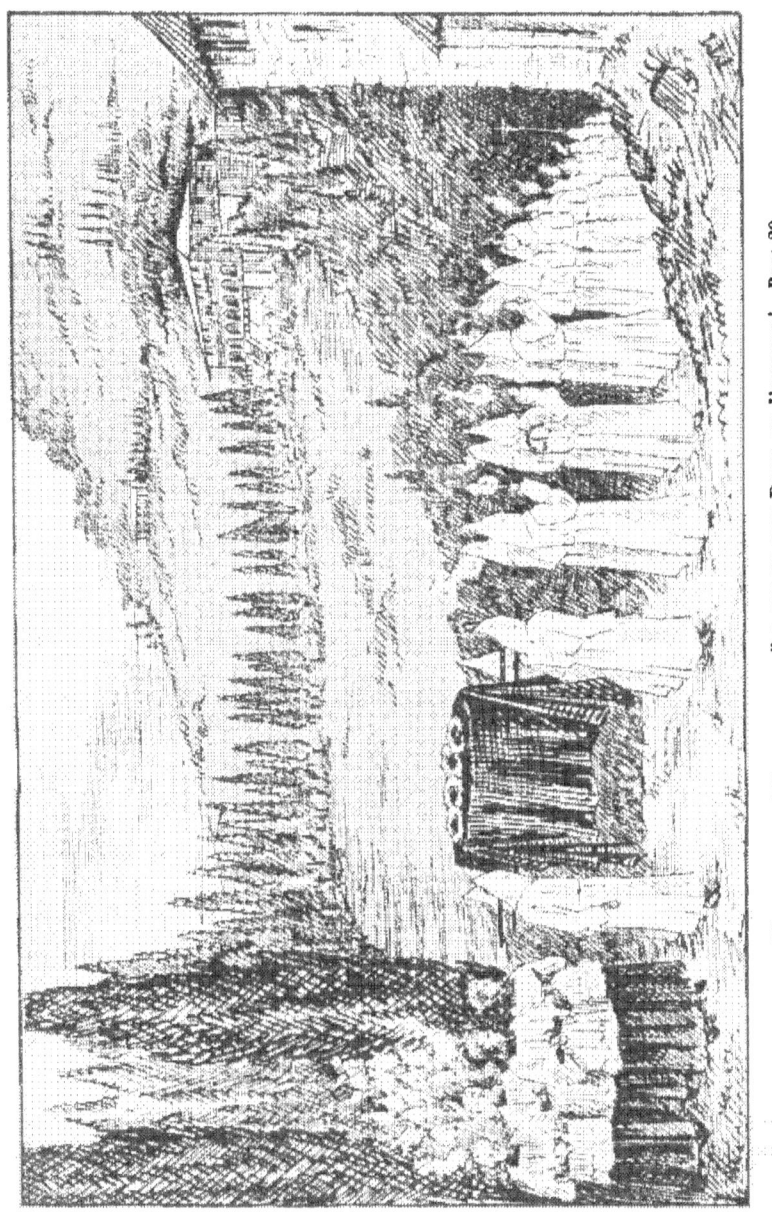

'THE WHITE-ROBED "MISERICORDIA" CAME IN THE DUSK OF EVENING.'—*Page* 29.

would not live to see the end of this ruin, proved true, and when Lidia bent over her mother's face the next morning it was white and motionless. She had been right indeed. The dim foreboding of her death that had prompted her to confide her daughter to the Marchese Vanatelli's care had been verified. The soul of the Marchesa had received its summons from the God Who sent her to His world; perhaps her haughty spirit could not brook the great humiliation and ruin, or perhaps God, in His infinite mercy, had taken pity on the mother's awakening, and on her disappointment in her son.

The white-robed 'Misericordia' came in the dusk of evening to carry the Marchesa Donati to her last resting-place. They filed in long procession down the dark cypress avenue, the ghostly white figures with their burning torches and the Crucifix heading the procession. Very slowly they wended their way into the city below, whose lights from the Fiesole hill looked dim and flickering, through the quiet, almost deserted, streets, where only a few spectators stood aside to watch the procession go by, and lifted their hats or crossed themselves, thus paying their last tribute to the dead being carried to the grave.

They are buried so, the rich and poor, in Italy, hurried away in the dusk of evening to the earth of which they are a part.

CHAPTER III.

The day after her mother's death and funeral Lidia sat alone in the drawing-room of her home. Her pale face was whiter than ever, and her eyes were red with weeping. Her mother's death had been a terrible shock to her, for her affections were deep and lasting. It is true the natures of mother and daughter differed greatly in many ways, but they had the same strict sense of honour which was lacking in the son and brother. She sat alone, her hands clasped in front of her, trying to force back the tears, and thinking how she should act as her mother would wish. She had not seen Carlo since the day before. He had locked himself in his own room, and refused to see anyone. She was wondering when the Englishman would come to claim his money, and how she should meet him. At last, stifled by the rising sobs, she sprang to her feet and began walking up and down the room. Her mother's voice seemed everywhere, the handsome, aristocratic face and stately walk, but though she heard and saw these visions, the scene of the previous night was ever before her eyes: the procession of white-robed figures, the flaring torches winding down the road to the weird, monotonous chant. There was no one to whom she could go in her distress. Contessa Mirandoli, her cousin in Switzerland, had been telegraphed to that morning, but there was no knowing when an answer would arrive. Lidia knew Giulia would come herself if that were possible, but she might easily be prevented. There was the Marchese Vanutelli. Had he been in Florence she would have asked him to come up to Fiesole immediately. Lidia did not remember the time when she would not have turned for help to their friend, whom from her earliest childhood she had been taught to look upon as one of themselves; but her mother had told her he was in Sicily, and she did not know his address.

Her mother's other friends in Florence were almost strangers to her, as she very rarely saw them. During her summer holidays her mother and Carlo with herself always left Fiesole for the mountains, and would return to Florence while the town was still empty. Neither was she accustomed to meet them during the winter, for the Marchesa seldom, if ever, brought her daughter forward, and, besides, Lidia knew that these friends had more genial occupations than looking after a ruined family.

'O Dio mio! what can I do?' she cried.

She was very young, and just out of a convent, thrown suddenly into poverty with her one brother, who was as good as no protector.

Albina came in, considerably subdued at that moment. There was a gentleman; he wished to see the Signor Marchese, but—— And the servant paused, recalling the sharp reproof she had received when she had last tried to open Carlo's door.

'Is it the Signor Inglese?' cried Lidia.

'Yes, signorina; he came here once before when the Marchesa—— O Dio mio! Dio mio!' she exclaimed, breaking into violent sobs.

'Oh, please do not cry!' entreated Lidia; 'I must not, and you will make me. I will see the signore.'

'Oh, la Marchesa—so beautiful, so stately!' sobbed the excited servant, unheeding; 'no one was like her.'

With a desperate effort for self-control her young mistress ordered her to show the signore upstairs. But there was no need for the injunction; Mr. Treherne already stood in the doorway. Albina cried 'Santa Vergine!' on espying him, and vanished.

Lidia remained motionless in the middle of the room. The man who now confronted her, and who held the fortune of her family in his hands, was tall and broad-shouldered, somewhat inclined to corpulency, and long past middle age. He was attired in a rather startling suit of checks, and a pugaree was twisted round his hat. He had a kindly, good-natured face, with iron-gray hair and beard, and altogether was very unlike the hard creditor Lidia had expected to see.

'Signor Trerni?' she said, able to speak at last, and giving an odd Italian sound to the English name.

'That is it,' replied Mr. Treherne, in his own language; 'I hope you understand English, madam; I don't speak Italian. I came to see the Marchese. Pardon me for intruding on you.'

'My brother is—is not able to come down,' she said, in pretty broken-English. 'I speak your language a little; I trust you will understand me, and hope you will pardon us for—for remaining in your house. My mother—my mother died yesterday.'

Mr. Treherne was much shocked. The stately presence of the Marchesa Donati had greatly impressed him, and he hardly realized the young girl's words.

'I am deeply grieved!' he exclaimed; 'I had no idea of this, or I should never have intruded upon you.'

'She died yesterday—suddenly,' replied the daughter in a low voice; 'but I am glad you have come, signore. We mean to leave this to you and—and go to Quaracchi.'

'Leave this to me!' repeated Mr. Treherne, rather bewildered. 'I don't understand.'

'Oh, signore,' cried Lidia, clasping her hands, 'my brother's debt to you is very great! We cannot pay—we have not the money. It was the wish of my mother you should take the villa.'

'I could not think of such a thing!' said the old gentleman quickly. 'What! I turn you out of your house for a mere bet made privately between your brother and myself! I——'

'Signore,' she interrupted, 'it is your house. We give this instead of money. It was my mother's wish.'

'Nonsense, nonsense!' exclaimed Mr. Treherne. 'I am very sorry I ever made the bet, and will now tell you the truth about it, madam. I wished to give the young fellow—your brother is he not?—a lift. His mother was not made for poverty. I saw he was going downhill pretty fast, and I was as sure as possible he would win. It was the only means I could think of to help him, and I could afford it. I wish to Heaven I had hit upon some other plan!'

'It was very kind of you,' faltered Lidia, the crimson flush that spread over her face being the only sign of the pride beneath the gentle exterior. 'What you have said proves the house to be more than ever yours. You would have paid my brother had you lost, and he must do the same.'

'But, good heavens!' exclaimed the Englishman, horror-struck at the idea that after all the pale girl before him meant what she said, 'do you expect me to turn you out of house and home?'

'No—no, do not fear,' she answered; 'we will go to our podere, and work there to pay what we still owe. Our podere is at Quaracchi, outside Florence.'

'I think,' said Mr. Treherne in a quieter tone, 'that I had better see your brother. I came, in fact, to tell him I wished the debt cancelled.'

'It was very kind of you,' she replied, the flush deepening; 'and I thank you, signore, for the gift we can never, never accept. We owe you this money; we must pay it to save our honour.'

'It is senseless pride!' exclaimed Mr. Treherne abruptly; 'I am a plain-spoken man, madam, and I must settle this business with your brother. He will see things as I do, I am sure.'

'Signore, it is an insult to offer us our house as a gift,' she answered. 'How can we accept it and save our honour? We cannot live on what ought to be yours. It is God's will the Madonna has not seen fit to pray that Carlo might win the race.'

'It is always the Madonna with you Italians,' said the old gentleman testily.

'The Madonna is the Mother of God,' she answered — 'after God, the one most loved and reverenced.'

'Hum!' said Mr. Treherne shortly. 'I have to return to England this evening, madam. I should like to see your brother before I start.'

'Oh, signore!' she cried, 'let it remain as I have said; I pray you do not speak of it to Carlo. It was my mother's wish. Before she died she explained to me how everything must be arranged.'

Mr. Treherne did not reply at once. He felt an odd sensation in his throat that checked his utterance for a moment.

'At least, madam,' he said respectfully, 'you will stay a week longer in the house. I will send out my son to arrange matters, as I am unable to remain to do so myself. It will give me great pleasure if you will consent.'

'Then we will stay that time,' she answered gravely. 'And, signore, you will please me by not—not speaking of this to Carlo, my brother. I will tell him you have been here, and how all has been arranged.'

Mr. Treherne understood what she meant. He had gained sufficient insight into Carlo Donati's character to know how vastly different it was from his mother's.

'I will obey you,' he answered; 'and believe me, I am deeply grieved at the turn affairs have taken. In my anxiety to be of service to you, I fear I have only given offence.'

The words were a reproach to Lidia. She held out her little hand to him.

'Doubtless, I am too proud, signore,' she said; 'but I act according to my mother's wishes: she intended to arrange it as I have done. If I have been discourteous, signore, I beg your pardon.'

'It is nothing—nothing,' he said hastily. 'Good-bye now, child, and let me know through my son if I can help you in any way. He will act in my stead if you will let him.'

'Thank you very much,' answered Lidia gratefully, yet with a touch of pride in her voice she could not quite conceal; 'it is very kind of you.'

'Ho! what senseless pride!' exclaimed Mr. Treherne to himself, as he walked down the avenue, away from the Villa Donati; 'wouldn't accept help if she were dying, I believe, and such a mite too—a mere child! I wonder how Frank and the Italian Countess will get on. Badly, I reckon. I am really sorry. I meant to do the lad a good turn more for his mother's sake than his own; she was not made for poverty. Poor soul! she went off suddenly enough.'

* * * * *

It was only natural Carlo should be angry when he heard how his sister had arranged matters with his English friend. But Lidia had not expected to be called selfish for what she had done, and it distressed her very much to hear Carlo say she had condemned him to a life of humiliation and poverty. She reminded him of their mother's wish—nay, of her positive command that the villa should go towards paying the debt. They could surely work. She had her painting; there were several who had said she could earn a living by it, and perhaps Carlo would also do something. Carlo was horrified — let all Florence know of their ruin and poverty? No! they must continue at Quaracchi the same kind of life they had been accustomed to lead at Fiesole. They would sell some of the furniture of the old farm-house, but keep on the carriages and horses.

Ah! the carriages and horses—that acknowledged sign of wealth, the pride of Carlo's heart! What mattered the privations they endured at home? Let them starve between bare walls, thought he, if they might still say a carriage and pair were at their disposal. To give up these would mean to lower himself in the estimation of his friends, and that he could not endure.

What! face them a self-confessed beggar, where he had been among the richest and most courted? It was impossible! Why not go at once to Quaracchi and sell the furniture as quietly as possible? It was very natural they should wish for retirement after their mother's death. If Lidia could make use of her painting to **earn money, of course it** would be an assistance, **and she must** economize in the **household.**

Lidia did not understand why there should be less talk if they sold the furniture instead of the horses; but she heard the selfish plans in silence, and said she would try to arrange everything as he wished.

CHAPTER IV.

Many visits of condolence for the death of the Marchesa Donati were paid at the Fiesole villa. Lidia saw no one. Besides knowing little of her mother's friends, she felt too sad to meet strange faces. She used to watch the grand carriages drive down the avenue, and wonder if the owners had to stint themselves to keep them. The week drew to a close. Lidia had tried to make Carlo tell her of the sale at Quaracchi, but he would only say it was all right and she was not to worry him. The Contessa Mirandoli had written from Switzerland, much distressed at the terrible blow of her aunt's death.

Her husband had been very ill; there had been delicacies to buy and bills to pay, they could not at once come to Florence, though they wished much to be near Lidia; but as soon as was possible they would leave the country the Contessa was by no means enchanted with. Lidia cried very much over the letter, so full of kind sympathy, and of a depth of feeling of which she had never thought the gay little Contessa capable. Since she received it, Lidia had felt more lonely than ever in longing for her cousin to come. Then there was Marchese Vanutelli. He had not returned to Florence, and though she had asked Carlo to find out where he was, no one knew his address. But he was expected home very soon, having only intended to stay away a week.

How Lidia longed for his return, knowing he would set everything right! Then, a moment after the wish, she was accusing herself of cowardice in trying to shirk her duty by leaving it to another to fulfil.

Carlo had gone down to Florence one afternoon, and Lidia was on the terrace sewing. The air was warm and peaceful; below lay the city in bright sunshine. Whenever she raised her head, the height of San Miniato, where her mother was buried, met her gaze. Lower down to the left was San Salvatore, surrounded by stately cypresses. She would have to leave it all very soon now for Quaracchi in the plain, among vineyards and olive-groves. The hill where her mother lay buried would be hidden from her. Her mother! Lidia closed her eyes, and seemed to see the tall and graceful figure with the beautiful face before her.

Albina came up to her mistress and roused her suddenly. There was a gentleman in the *salon*; he wished to see the Contessina.

'Marchese?' faltered Lidia, her heart beating with excitement.

Albina knew directly who was meant. From her childhood there had been only one Marchese to Lidia, and, indeed, she always spoke of him as Marchese, till it had become her pet name for their old friend.

No; it was an Englishman.

Lidia started to her feet.

'Is not Carlo at home?' she exclaimed.

'Oh no, he is in Florence,' was the answer; 'he has left the Contessina alone. Here is the gentleman's card.'

Lidia hardly looked at it. She guessed immediately who had come to see her, and hesitated to advance.

'The Contessina need not be afraid,' said

Albina encouragingly; 'he is very good-looking—and young, too.'

Lidia went slowly towards the drawing-room. What if the son had not the father's kindliness?

Mr. Treherne came forward to meet her as she stepped in from the veranda. He was above middle height, of slighter build than his father, and his features were more regular, though the kindly expression was not there. In its place was a hard, searching look in his gray eyes, and though he was not more than seven or eight and twenty, his face had the suspicious, cynical look of a man of the world.

'I am speaking to——' he began, in an inquiring tone.

'Contessa Lidia Donati,' she answered, bowing nervously.

Mr. Treherne lifted his eyebrows in slight astonishment. He had not expected a child to come forward in answer to that name. From what his father had said, he imagined Carlo's sister to be a stately Italian lady who had rejected with disdain every offer of assistance. What pride could exist in the child before him? wondered Mr. Treherne. 'My father must have gone about the business badly;' and he set himself to achieve what his father had failed in. She looked as though she were much too frightened to refuse anything he might ask her to accept.

'You have come to see my brother, signore,' she said in English, and endeavouring to conquer her nervousness. 'He is in Florence. I am very sorry he is not here to meet you.'

'It is true I have business to settle with him,' he replied, with a slight emphasis on the last word, as though he wished her to understand it had nothing to do with her; 'but my father wished me to ask you if there is anything you would allow him to do for you.'

'No, indeed,' she answered; 'there is nothing. Please tell him he is very kind to think of me. To-morrow we go to Quaracchi, and I hope, signore, you will find the house to suit you.'

She spoke with a certain dignity that hid her shyness, and made Treherne waver in his decision that she was too young to be proud. She certainly could draw up her little figure and look independent. He began to wonder whether it was his father's fault, after all. Treherne was apt to be a disbeliever in honourable pride; he had treated his father's declaration that Carlo's sister was so proud she would not ask for a penny, even were she starving, with an incredulity that vexed the old man, who had told his son to go and see for himself if what he said was not true. And Treherne, like most young men, did not care to own he had been wrong, and that, whatever might be his opinion of his fellow-creatures in general, Lidia Donati was an exception to the rule.

'You cannot imagine how much this has grieved my father,' he said, 'having expected such a different result.'

'It was the will of God,' said the little Countess in a low voice, 'and therefore better as it is. Will you come out on the terrace to wait for my brother, signore? I can show you the view over Florence.'

Treherne was suddenly silenced. He could not broach the subject of cancelling the debt after hearing the proud tone of her voice. It was very strange. He was seldom disconcerted.

That he should be balked by a mere child made Treherne somewhat impatient, but he followed her without a word to the terrace, till they stood together looking over the blue Lucchese mountains and the rich Tuscan valley below.

'It is the will of God,' she murmured to herself in Italian, so low that her companion did not hear, only he guessed she was mourning over her lost home; and probably for the first time in his life Francis Treherne felt in the way and uncomfortable. He began to wish he had never come on this mission. Why could not his father have arranged everything before returning home, instead of leaving all the disagreeable part for his son to fulfil?

'Have you lived here all your life?' he asked suddenly, more for the sake of something to say than from any desire to know.

'Yes,' she answered; 'and if you live in the villa you will take care of it, will you not, signore? I am glad your father should have it, for he has been very kind to us, and will understand how much we love our home. You will let no one else live in it, will you?'

She looked at him with wistful, childish eyes, then on her home—on the yellow walls figured in quaint brown designs. Between the two hills the campanile of the Fiesole church above stood out against the clear blue sky.

'Yes, we will take care of it,' said Treherne, an odd mist coming before his eyes as he noticed the distress the child could not hide at having to leave her home.

Both were silent for a few moments. Treherne was looking over the valley below, when Lidia said nervously:

'Signore, please tell me, has your father told you to make any offer to my brother?'

'Any offer?' repeated Treherne, raising his eyebrows in affected astonishment, and with the tone of voice that generally silenced his questioners. Lidia, however, was too eager to be overawed.

'Yes,' she replied; 'when he came to see me he wished us to—to take it all back. We cannot do that. My mother wished everything to be paid. Do not ask Carlo, my brother, to accept anything.'

'You are afraid of his consenting,' he said

bluntly. Treherne was no man to mince matters; what he meant he said. 'I should ask him for that very reason. You are quite unfit, my father says, to be suddenly reduced to poverty. He had no idea things would have turned out so unfortunately. My business is entirely with your brother. You will allow me to wait for him.'

'What can a child like you know about such matters?' his voice and manner plainly said.

'Signore!' she exclaimed in a stifled voice, her face crimson, her little figure drawn up ever so slightly, though Treherne noticed the difference immediately, 'it is impossible! We are satisfied as we are. We go to our podere at Quaracchi, where there is all we need. We do not wish to live on the charity of others, however kind that charity may be.'

Yes, Treherne had to own his father had been in the right. There was no mistaking the determination in her eyes and voice as she answered him.

'Surely,' said Treherne, unable to suppress a sarcastic smile hovering round his mouth, 'such pride is contrary to your religion.'

'It is at least honourable,' she answered.

'Why should we live on charity when we can work for ourselves? I do not think God can be offended. I would rather suffer anything than be the cause of loss or injury to your father, who has been so kind to us. I am sure God will reward his charity, and I will ask the Madonna to pray for him.'

'Ah, yes,' said the young man; 'God and the Madonna—that is the Italian's religion.'

'You are of the English Church?' she asked timidly. 'I have heard of it. You will pardon me if I say it is a strange doctrine. There was an English girl at my convent, poverina; she never prayed to the Madonna or the saints. It was dreadful!'

'And still more dreadful not to pray to anyone, I suppose,' said Treherne, looking down at the little figure, and wondering what effect his words would have on her.

'Not to pray to anyone at all?' she echoed, knitting her brows with a puzzled air. 'Not to the good God Himself, signore?'

She looked doubtfully up at him.

'Exactly,' he answered; 'I mean one who prays neither to God, to the Madonna, nor to the saints.'

'Why?' she asked, with such childish wonder that Treherne smiled.

'Because he does not believe in them,' he answered, a little hastily.

'Then to whom does he pray?' asked Lidia, in a shocked voice, still with the wondering expression in her eyes.

'To no one, of course,' answered Treherne, impatient at her want of understanding, and returning to his former conclusion that she was only a child.

'To no one!' she echoed again. 'Then who will he thank for his being, for the beautiful earth, the valley and the hills?'

She pointed to the city as she spoke, and then to the distant Carrara mountains.

'They came by nature,' replied Treherne, beginning to feel amused at the earnest face of the little Countess and her utter ignorance of the world.

'Then Nature must be the god of such an unbeliever,' she said; 'he worships Nature.'

'No,' persisted the young man, smiling; 'he worships no one.'

'That is impossible,' she said; 'that is not in the nature of man. Where did he live whom you speak of? Did no one ever tell him of God, of the Madonna, or the saints?'

'Oh, he was taught,' replied Treherne carelessly, 'but he did not believe.'

'He set himself above those who taught him,' said the young girl gravely; 'then he worships himself, fancying he knows better than the millions who have gone before him.'

There was a moment's silence.

'I am afraid you do not understand,' said Treherne, thinking that, after all, it was waste of time to argue with a child like this. She shook her head very slowly.

'No, I do not,' she replied. 'I do not wish to do so.'

'If you had lived as many have,' he said, 'it would not seem hard. If you had seen countless numbers of your fellow-beings living a life of absolute misery, uncared for in the depths of poverty, then would the temptation come to you to ask, Where is the God they speak of that He does not come forward to help His creatures?'

It was very strange that, still thinking her only a child, he should speak to her like this.

'It is as you say, signore, a temptation,' she

replied; 'the Madonna will very soon drive that away if you ask her. It is sin that has brought misery and poverty into the world. Such misery as you speak of does not come to those who trust in God, only to those who never go to Him for help. Oh, signore, I cannot explain, but it seems very clear to me.'

'Some are blinded, I suppose,' he said; 'others are rudely awakened.'

'Indeed it is so,' she replied, misunderstanding him. 'Those are blinded who do not pray to God; those are rudely awakened who, when they die, come before Him Whose existence they have denied.'

Her brown eyes were lighted up with eagerness, and Lidia Donati looked lovely in spite of her thin, pale face; her hands were clasped on the parapet of the terrace; all her warm Italian nature was roused and showed itself in her words.

'You speak English very well,' said Treherne abruptly, after a short pause. 'How did you learn it?'

She coloured and smiled.

'At the convent,' she answered; 'there were several English girls there, and my mother was very fond of English: she often spoke it with me.'

'How old are you?' asked Treherne, still in the same abrupt voice.

Lidia drew back a little, and looked up at him, unmistakable surprise expressed in her eyes. This was not at all what she had been brought up to consider correct. Indeed, it now seemed to her she had been acting against the rules of *convenance* throughout the interview.

'I beg your pardon!' exclaimed Treherne, perceiving her astonishment, and coming to the conclusion he never afterwards gave up, that Lidia was not a child. 'I thought you were younger than you are.'

At that moment the Marchese Donati appeared suddenly at one of the windows of the drawing-room, and Lidia, bowing to Treherne, went away.

The Quaracchi Farm.—*Page 57.*

CHAPTER V.

A MONTH had passed since the Marchesa Donati's death. Lidia and her brother were at their Quaracchi farm, a rambling old two-storied house situated amidst vineyards and olive-trees, and it was here they had come to starve. Mr. Treherne had shut up the house on the Fiesole hill and gone back to England. They had heard nothing of him since his departure—a week after his arrival in Florence.

Carlo Donati still drove his carriage and pair into Florence, while his sister stayed at home, trying to make both ends meet, and worrying her life out over his unpaid bills. The horses were expensive. Lidia could not earn enough by painting to keep them and pay for real necessaries. The money for the furniture seemed to have gone a very little way. It is true she worked from morning till night, and had sold the picture she had finished at a much higher price than she had expected, but money was wanting.

Lidia was hurrying out of the little country church one Sunday morning among the crowd of peasants, all wearing their gaily-coloured handkerchiefs and the wonderful pearl necklaces kept as heirlooms in every well-to-do *contadino* family round Florence. She wanted to get home quickly to her painting, and though she would have gladly lingered awhile in the peaceful country road between the vineyards, she turned swiftly up the narrow lane that led to her own home.

The *cicade* were chattering noisily in the olive-trees around—so noisily, indeed, that Lidia did not hear the rapid footsteps behind her. It was only when her own name was called that she heard and turned round. Her face, wistful and grave enough before, changed suddenly into one of delighted surprise.

'Oh, Marchese! Marchese!' just in the same voice she used as a child to greet him when she had not seen him for a long time, only the last word ended in what sounded very like a sob. Marchese Vanutelli's exceedingly grave face hardly relaxed as he silently took her hand.

The sight of him brought back many memories to Lidia. The last time she had seen him was on her birthday, when she had been allowed to spend the day and night at Fiesole with her mother and brother. The Marchese had come up to see them in the afternoon, as he always did on her birthday, and had given his present. He was such an old friend of the family that this was allowed.

The little pearl earrings did not belong to Lidia any more now. With many silent tears she had parted with them, as she had with many of her other treasures. Money was so scarce when they came to Quaracchi.

'You did not write to tell me, child!' he exclaimed at last.

'No, I could not; I did not know the address,' answered Lidia in a low voice, 'and I expected you to come every day.'

'My business kept me longer than I thought it would,' he said; 'I had no idea anything had gone wrong with you. I received no letter recalling me, so concluded all had been arranged satisfactorily. I come and find everything in this terrible state — povera piccina!'

And the grave face softened considerably as he looked at the child who had been confided to his care. Lidia glanced up at him, a trusting light shining in her soft eyes as though she knew everything would be easier now. He walked on beside her.

'It—it was very sudden,' she faltered. 'We had no idea she—she was unwell the night before; we——'

'You need not tell me more,' he said, seeing her white, distressed face; 'I understand how it must have happened. And you have left the villa?'

Lidia went through the whole sad story. The Marchese was greatly shocked. He had received no news of the race that had been lost; neither had he any idea the Fiesole villa was given to the Englishman in payment of the debt. He bitterly reproached himself for not having left his business in Sicily and returned sooner to see if all was right with the family to which he was so attached. The poor child had had to bear her cross alone without the protector to whom her mother had entrusted her only a few days before she died.

'How thoughtless of me!' he exclaimed, half to himself.

'It is all right now you have returned, Marchese,' said Lidia; 'and how could you know what was happening when you were away? Had you been at home, I am sure you would have been the first to come forward to help us in our sorrow.'

'But I ought to have written!' he answered quickly. 'The fact was, I had such trouble with the property I forgot everyone but myself. What are you doing now? Tell me everything, Lidia. Has Carlo found any employment?'

She looked up into his face in astonishment. Carlo work! After her brother had treated the idea with such wonder and disdain, she herself had begun to look on it in the same light. She shook her head, half smiling that the fine handsome Carlo should so demean himself.

'Oh, no, of course not!'

The Marchese did not quite understand her surprise; he set it down to another cause.

'Why not?' he asked. 'I should have thought plenty would have been ready to take him on trial. There is Frattigiani, the banker. I know he has several—— Why, child, what makes you look so astonished?'

'Carlo does not work,' she answered, looking up at him. 'You surely do not expect him to, Marchese?'

Her companion looked more mystified than ever. The idea that any man would not make an effort to support his sister and save her from the life of poverty, such as he knew the Donatis must be subject to now, never occurred to him. How on earth could they live? Had Lidia lost some of the good sense the Marchese had admired in her even when she was only a child? How could she expect to pay debts that must be accumulating every day? He looked down at Lidia, who was still smiling. After all, she was only a child, unaccustomed to the ways of poverty. He must try and explain.

'Not expect him to!' he repeated; 'of course I do! Who is to work for you and support you if not your brother? You know, Lidia, debts will accumulate when you do not pay them, and make your life a burden. Carlo——'

'Oh, I,' interrupted Lidia—'I work, you know. There is my painting, and though expenses are—are rather high, we try—I try to do my best.'

The sentence was begun cheerfully enough, as though she wished to make light of her troubles, but the brave young voice quivered at the end. The change on the Marchese's face was instantaneous. With a flash he understood how things were. Had not the mother foreseen that Carlo would oppress his sister by his selfishness? But this the Marchese had not deemed possible from any man.

Gifted with a strict sense of honour himself, he could not understand or realize the lack of it in others; and this act of the brother in allowing his young sister to work for him, thus laying all the burden of poverty upon her, was repulsive to him. For some moments they walked on together in silence, Lidia now and then glancing timidly up at him, as though she knew he disapproved of what had been told him.

Not until they arrived at the Quaracchi farm, and had stopped in front of a little wooden door in the stone wall that separated the vineyard from the road, did Marchese Vanutelli speak.

'This cannot be allowed to go on,' he said, frowning. 'I had no idea Carlo could have behaved in such a manner. I must speak to him.'

'Oh no, Marchese!' exclaimed Lidia; 'Carlo says he is not fit for work, that——'

'Does he think you are?' asked the Marchese sharply. 'No, I must see him. Is he at home?'

'Yes; but, oh!' she cried, hanging back on his arm, and thinking, child as she was in many ways, to keep him back, 'do not say anything to him! Please come in here and listen to me.'

She opened the wooden door that led into the olive-grove, where the green vines hung like graceful garlands from olive-tree to olive-tree. The *cicale* sounded as deafening as ever in the branches overhead. To the left the broad shady veranda stretched along the façade of the old white farm-house. As she closed the little green door, Lidia turned to her companion.

'I have spoken of it to him,' she said; 'but he has not been brought up to work, Marchese, and it will be so hard for him to go into Florence, where everyone knows him.'

'Those are weak and cowardly excuses,' interrupted the Marchese. 'Were he in bad health, and so unable to tire himself working, I could understand it; but how a man can allow his sister to keep him in idleness, I cannot conceive.'

Lidia was silent. She began playing nervously with her Prayer-Book. The Marchese looked at her; she was very pale and thin, as though she were indeed overworked. He had misjudged the child; she understood as well as he did how necessary it was to keep out of debt. She had worried herself, he could see, for her face had regained the wistful, grave expression. What had been his promise to the mother? How had he looked after her?

'It cannot be allowed to go on,' he said firmly. 'What have you been doing to keep your brother in idleness?'

'I—I paint,' she answered. 'And the picture I finished the other day was bought sooner than might have been expected. It is a little hard sometimes when I think of the Fiesole villa, but mamma wished it so. The Signor Inglese wanted me to take it all back, which was very kind of him, and when his son came to Florence he was—was rather angry, I think, with me for being so proud.'

And Lidia smiled up into her old friend's face, but the Marchese felt a strange tightening in his heart as he met the wistful gaze of her brown eyes.

'Angry with you!' he repeated. 'Did not Carlo arrange everything?'

Oh! what had she done? Unwittingly let out what she wanted to keep most secret even from their friend—Carlo's reluctance to obey his mother's wishes. The Marchese's quick eye detected her hesitation.

'Bimba mia, why do you not tell me everything? Your mother confided you to my care before I left Florence. Then, God knows, I thought there was no need for my promise, though I gave it, to look after you and see you were happy. You must not overwork yourself, you hear, child? Why not tell me all that has happened, and whatever has distressed you, that I may make your life as smooth as it should be?'

'You were always so kind to us, Marchese,' she answered earnestly; 'there is nothing much to tell you. Carlo arranged all about the sale of a few of her things before we came here, and he saw Signor Trerni's son. Poverty is harder for him than it is for me, Marchese; at the convent we always lived very simply.'

Her companion's eyes were misty as he saw her earnestness and desire to shield her brother from all blame. But he was not the less angry with Carlo for his utter selfishness and want of self-respect. Lidia hesitated after her last words as though she wished to say more; then with crimson face she put her hands to her ears to show him her earrings were gone. The Marchese's eyes followed the direction she pointed out, and he smiled.

'They—I had to sell them,' she faltered, not knowing he had found out already what had become of them.

'Yes,' he said, still smiling, 'and here they are.'

He took the little morocco case from his pocket as he spoke and held it out to her. Lidia started back, too bewildered for words, yet childish delight shining in her eyes at seeing her treasure again. She looked up at him wondering if he was offended at her parting with them, though it had cost her many a bitter pang.

'You sent them to the shop where I bought them,' he said, much amused at her bewilderment. 'When I arrived in Florence I went there to get some other small thing to bring you, and while choosing I came across these. Well, bimba, they are very ordinary little earrings, and yet I recognised them.'

'It is true I sent them there,' said Lidia in a low voice, her eyes fixed on the box, though not offering to take it. 'Oh, Marchese, I had to! You will forgive me!'

'Am I to keep them?' he asked, still holding out the case patiently, 'or will they not be claimed by their owner?'

Lidia flushed crimson, half in delight, half in surprise, but the colour soon faded away.

'They—they are too rich for me now,' she faltered. 'I do not even wear such things, Marchese, but I do not want to offend you.'

She looked up at him, and then half stretched out her hand.

'What am I to do with them?' he said. 'They will look prettier on you, child, than on anyone else.' And he put the little morocco case in her hand.

'Then you will let me give you something—is it not so, Marchese?' she asked, with childish trust in her eyes as she looked up at him.

'What is it?' asked the Marchese.

'You will take one,' said Lidia, holding out a little pearl. 'Please do! I cannot wear them yet so soon—so soon after her death, and it will remind you how kind you have been to me; you know, Marchese, you always forget how good you are.' She was watching his face eagerly. 'I shall have the best of the bargain,' she went on quite merrily he was glad to hear, 'in keeping the box.'

Marchese Vanutelli stretched out his hand half mechanically; he saw her put one of her much-loved little treasures into his keeping, saw her flushed, eager face, the light in her childish eyes. Everything else—the festoons of green leaves hanging from tree to tree, the old farmhouse with its whitewashed walls shining in the sun behind her—was blotted out from his eyes.

Very quietly he took the hand that had given the present and kissed it reverently, while Lidia smiled. He had often done so before, and called her a wise little woman of the world, so it was no new thing to her, but somehow to him it was different: up at the Fiesole villa he had kissed the hand of a child; here, under the olives in the old Quaracchi farm, it was the hand of the one who in a very short moment had filled the first place in his thoughts, not because of his promise to her mother, but because he loved her.

'Now, is not that quite right?' asked Lidia, little guessing what had come of her present and the way it had been offered, 'and thank you so much, Marchese.'

'Must I not thank you too?' he asked, trying to rouse himself, and not altering his manner. 'I will always keep it. And now, child, I will go and see Carlo. Piccina, are you afraid I shall be unjust to him?' he asked, almost reproachfully, as she made as though to prevent him from going forward.

'No, no,' she answered; 'only I wish—I wish I had never told you. He is very quick-tempered; I would not have him say anything to grieve you.'

She was still the same lovable little girl who would run to meet him in the cypress avenue of the Fiesole villa. Many a scene rose up before his eyes of the child Lidia; now she was standing beside him, the one he loved best in the world.

'Do not be anxious,' he said; 'even if Carlo loses his temper, it is not likely I shall lose mine. Shall we go in?'

Lidia followed her companion, trying to hide her anxiety in order not to trouble him. They ascended the old stone steps of the veranda together.

Carlo was sitting in a room that opened out on to the terrace. He started up on seeing who it was that stood on the threshold ready to greet him, and Lidia slipped away to her studio.

Carlo did not lose his temper. He was too much taken aback. Never before had he seen his old friend so roused out of himself; and as the grave eyes rested upon him with an unusually stern expression, he felt, indeed, a twinge of remorse, and was silent before his reprover.

But he offered to make no amends for his past conduct; he resolved on no different path for the future. How could he, accustomed as he was to a life of ease, give himself up to daily work? How could he, the Marchese Donati, face his acquaintances in Florence as a banker's clerk? No, he could not do it!

Marchese Vanutelli went up to him at last, and laid his hand kindly on the young man's shoulder.

'Conquer self, my boy,' he said. 'Perhaps I have spoken too severely, and have not sufficiently considered the position you are in. I will gladly give you the amount you require at present, but it would be foolishly indulgent if I kept you in idleness. I trust you to see about an occupation as soon as possible. At first you may earn very little, but you must come to me when you are in difficulties—will you not, Carlo?'

The Marchese drew out his pocket-book as he spoke. He hesitated in laying the banknotes on the table, as though he were afraid of hurting the young man's feelings; but Carlo was too much in want of money to make objections to any of his friend's plans.

'I will leave you these,' said the Marchese, relieved to find Carlo did not take offence, and altering his tone of reproof to that of friendliness. 'Try and conquer self, Carlo; it is your worst enemy.'

Marchese Vanutelli held out his hand to the young man, who had risen and tried to stammer out some thanks as he saw the money and realized how much might be done with it.

'No, no,' answered his friend, smiling; 'you must not speak your thanks, but act them by doing what I ask you—will you not, Carlo?'

When Carlo promised, I do not doubt he had every intention of remaining true to his word. He was touched by the disinterested kindness of their friend. But, as the Marchese had said, self was a terrible enemy; it had a strong hold on the young man; nothing but an immense effort would shake it off.

'May time and fortune bring you good luck!' said the Marchese kindly. 'Do not hesitate to come to me if you want anything, Carlo, for yourself or your sister. Good-bye, my boy!'

He went down the steps of the veranda alone. Carlo had remained half stupefied at the sudden good fortune that brought their friend to him when he was in a particularly embarrassed position.

Marchese Vanutelli paused before the little wooden door he had entered with Lidia. A voice, calling 'Marchese, Marchese!' made him turn, and Lidia, breathless from running downstairs, overtook him. She was completely covered in a great apron, and ran up with her palette and brush, which she had been in too great a hurry to lay aside on catching sight of him from her studio window, leaving the house.

'Oh, why did you not call me?' she exclaimed reproachfully. 'I wanted so much to know what Carlo said.'

Carlo had promised to work, the Marchese answered; but his thoughts were very far from Carlo as his eyes wandered up and down the little artist's figure.

'Why are you dressed up like that?' he added, smiling.

'I am painting,' she answered. 'Oh, Marchese, how good of you to ask Carlo! I have tried so much to get him to consent. Mamma would have wished it, and it will give Carlo something to do; but oh, Marchese, it will be very hard for him to work in Florence, where he is well known.'

'Would you find it hard if it was to support one you loved?' asked her companion, a little gravely. 'It is not an honourable pride that makes one shirk his evident duty, is it, child?'

Lidia did not answer, but the Marchese knew very well what she thought.

'You must not overtax your strength,' he said, looking at the palette and brush. 'You are not fit for hard work, and the young must enjoy themselves. You have borne a great deal bravely, piccina!'

The Marchese spoke in a protecting, almost tender, voice.

'Thank you so much,' she answered. 'Mamma indeed was right when she asked you to take care of us. She knew how good you were.'

She spoke so earnestly that the Marchese's eyes grew dim as they looked at her. Carlo had walked mechanically on to the veranda while they were speaking, and there he caught sight of his sister, as she was offering her hand to their friend. A thought, and not at all a disagreeable one, suddenly struck him. After all, Marchese Vanutelli was not so very old—not too old by any means to choose a wife; and if—if it could be arranged, all Carlo's difficulties would be at an end. It was not likely a man would let his brother-in-law live in poverty when he was wealthy enough to support him.

Unsuspecting Lidia opened the door of the vineyard to let their friend out.

'You will come very often to see us, will you not?' she said almost wistfully as he bade her good-bye. 'You help me so much, Marchese!'

He helped her so much! Should he tell her how he longed to do so all his life, how he would give up all to take care of and love her as her mother would wish?

No, not yet. She might come to him out of gratitude alone; better wait a little while, for she was still young, and not trouble her yet with his wishes. Lidia did not dream of what was passing in his mind; nay, it even seemed to her he bade good-bye more quietly than usual.

She waved her hand to him, smiling, as he walked down the white road. He had almost forgotten that once—ay, even a few hours before—the little figure standing in the doorway was not all in all to him. Marchese Vanutelli lived alone; he had no one else in the world to care for or love.

Before the thought of her happiness all others should give way; he had promised her mother so. He kept that promise till he died. But how he was able to keep it no one knew but himself, and God Who helped the brave and noble heart.

CHAPTER VI.

CARLO had recovered from his surprise in the evening, so much so as to be out of temper now that no other course seemed open to him except work.

His sister was brighter than ever, though there was that terrible page of figures to add up of yesterday's expenses. The figures would not stay still before her eyes, but kept dancing up and down till the columns seemed like blots on the white paper. It was no good: Lidia could not make the figures come less, however often she might add them up.

Carlo was pretending to read his paper, so that he might not be expected to take any notice of his sister's exertions. He had not condescended to answer her exclamations of delight about Marchese Vanutelli's sudden arrival. Except for the present of money, Carlo could have done very well without their friend. What he had urged showed that the Marchese had a great deal more consideration for the sister than he had for the brother, so Carlo decided he had been treated unjustly. He would have to go into Florence as a poor clerk, and be probably cut by all his friends; while Lidia stayed at home, allowing him to bear the brunt of Florentine gossip. Why did Vanutelli want to come meddling with their affairs? Why could he not mind his own business?

Lidia had probably been complaining—it was like her—Carlo began to grumble out loud. She had harped on her favourite subject —the horses. It was the one luxury he allowed himself, and that she grudged him. While she was comfortable at home, she expected her brother to trudge about on foot.

'Oh, Carlo!' she exclaimed, greatly distressed at his reproaches.

The room was bare enough, with the plain wooden tables and chairs; her studio, too, where she spent her days, was cheerless. There seemed little comfort about the old farmhouse for her to enjoy, but Lidia could say no more, and she bent her head again over the row of dancing figures.

'I tell you what,' exclaimed Carlo, a little remorseful, as he saw his sister's pale face, and remembered who it was that bore all the worry of the bills without a murmur: 'you want an outing, Lidia. You must drive into Florence with me; it will do you good.'

She shook her head, unable to reply.

'How thoughtless you are!' he exclaimed; 'you have never shown your face in Florence since we left Fiesole. How can I answer all the questions put to me about you? You cannot remain in retirement all your life because of our mother's death. Why not go immediately into a convent?'

'You can say I do not wish to see anyone,' she answered; 'that I prefer quiet, which is very true. We cannot go on living like this, Carlo; but you have promised Marchese to work, have you not? It will be all right. We shall be quite happy with a little more money and less expenses, and you will have something to occupy you.'

'Yes,' muttered Carlo; 'I am to give up my few comforts for a miserly whim.'

'It is not a whim,' she answered. 'Do you think those you call your friends would not find out everything sooner or later?—that the Fiesole home was given away to pay a debt? Padre Antonio told me yesterday Signor Trerni had sent his servants to arrange the villa, and when he comes he will undeceive everyone. I do not know what you have told the people of Florence, or how you have satisfied them about our leaving the house. They will doubtless learn the truth from Signor Trerni.'

'That shall not be!' cried Carlo, starting up from his chair. 'He is bound not to—— The son has arranged. He knows if he does he will see little of the debt.'

Lidia clasped her hands.

'Carlo!' she exclaimed, her voice shrill and sharp, 'have you deceived me? I told you to find out the value of our house and pay the rest. Madonna mia! do we still owe money to the Signor Inglese?'

Carlo rose in anger — the anger that a coward always takes refuge in.

'What a fuss you women do make about a trifle!' he exclaimed, going towards the door.

'Then you did not pay?' she asked, rising too. 'We are still debtors to Signor Trerni?'

'This is nonsense!' cried her brother. 'Treherne arranged it all; his son told me he would not take what remained. He said I was to keep it to make you comfortable.'

'And you came to me saying you had done as I asked you,' said Lidia, unable to hide the bitterness she felt. 'You deceived me!'

'How dare you speak so to me in my own house!' cried Carlo, with flushed cheeks and excited voice. 'I will not submit!'

He did not wait for an answer, but left the room, banging the door after him.

Lidia sank down in a chair, her head falling on her hands. For some time she remained motionless. Perhaps she was too proud and sensitive. We suppose so. There is no perfect human character, but she could not understand this terrible slavery to self.

She took up her candle at last, and went slowly upstairs to her room, which communicated with the studio. The unfinished picture stood on the easel. It represented a peasant girl kneeling before a shrine of the Madonna.

But Lidia could see nothing; blurred and

blotted figures seemed to dance before the *contadina's* pleading face. She turned away slowly and went back to her room.

* * * * *

Lidia was working at her picture very early the next day. Albina, who was their only servant now, except the coachman, brought up her mistress's breakfast, a piece of bread and a bunch of dried grapes. Being a very privileged servant, Lidia's friend and confidante, she was almost as much elated as her mistress at the sudden arrival of Marchese Vanutelli, and she stood beside Lidia, unwilling to leave her alone.

'But, signorina, eat more,' she urged.

'No, that is enough,' answered Lidia, handing her back the plate. 'See that Beppo has the carriage ready for the Signor Marchese: he is going into Florence this morning. That is all.'

'The Contessina works too much,' said Albina with decision. 'She——'

Albina did not finish her sentence, for the Signor Marchese walked in himself at that moment, and Albina wisely withdrew, while Lidia greeted her brother. The remembrance of yesterday's events had not served to sweeten Carlo's temper, yet something must be done, or Marchese Vanutelli might see fit to proclaim to all Florence the poverty of the Donatis. He would go into the town that morning, he told Lidia somewhat sulkily, and see what could be done. He hoped she was satisfied now that she had made his life a burden. It did seem hard on a brother that his sister should plan with a friend to deprive him of his few luxuries.

'I hope you will find something,' Lidia answered, quietly taking no notice of the reproaches, though they distressed her none the less. 'Mother would have wished it, Carlo.'

Well, Carlo would see about it, perhaps that day. He left the studio and entered the carriage waiting for him. In no enviable state of mind, he hardly condescended to lift his hat to the old Franciscan friar who, as Carlo drove past, nodded and smiled to him.

He was very feeble, this white-haired monk. Albina stood in the doorway as he came up to the Quaracchi farm.

'Good-day,' said Padre Antonio, his kind

and wrinkled face beaming with smiles. 'Can I see the signorina?'

Oh, of course; she was up in the studio, Albina declared; she never left it for anyone.

Padre Antonio followed her slowly up the stairs, for he was much troubled with rheumatism. When Lidia saw him standing in the doorway, she rose to greet him, delighted. Albina lingered too; she had several grievances to air. There was the Contessina working herself to the bone, while the Signor Marchese did nothing. Scusi! but she must speak. Did not Padre Antonio think it disgraceful?

The old friar shook his head as a sign he agreed with Albina; and before Lidia could speak the good-natured servant rattled off again. Marchese Vanutelli had been the day before; he would set everything right, Albina knew, for he was always so fond of the Contessina, and it was certainly time to do so. A month had passed without any change; her mistress always worrying, and so unaccustomed as she was to poverty——

Lidia laughingly pushed her out of the room at last, then turned to the old friar, who still looked grave.

'Do not be severe on him,' she exclaimed; 'it is going to be all right now. He promised Marchese to work.'

Padre Antonio brightened.

'Ah! I am very glad Marchese Vanutelli has spoken to him,' he said. 'You would never let me do so, child. But who can teach the young, if not the old?'

'Carlo is very changed,' she said in a low voice. 'I do not understand. He very seldom goes to church now.'

The old man looked at her sadly.

'It is the spirit of the age to scoff at holy things,' he replied. 'Your good mother kept much of this from you when you returned home for your holidays. This change in your brother grieves me sorely. I taught him when he was a child. I fear I have failed in my work.'

There was a pause; then Lidia said wistfully:

'You will pray for him, Padre?'

'Certainly, child,' was the answer; 'the rest we will leave in God's hands.'

'God will not refuse to hear our prayers,' she said. 'I do not like to speak of it to him: it seems to make him worse.'

'No; in these cases we must only pray' said Padre Antonio gravely. 'To speak of it to those we wish to convert has sometimes a bad result. But something ought to be done to prevent you from ruining your health, child.'

'I am not ruining my health,' expostulated Lidia.

'All this to keep up appearances,' exclaimed Padre Antonio pityingly. 'I am glad Marchese Vanutelli has returned, for Carlo may listen more willingly to him than he would to me. Already I hear people beginning to wonder why Marchese Donati never sees his friends in his house, as he is ready enough to go to Florence and drive about, which shows he is no longer in retirement for his mother's death. The truth would come out sooner or later. We could not help it.'

Then Lidia, with her brother's reproaches still in her ears, tried to make excuses. After all, Carlo had so few luxuries now, compared to what he was accustomed to, and it was very hard for him to go into Florence and work for his living before all his friends.

But Padre Antonio was indignant. Had she ruined her brother, that she should bear all the disagreeables? No. It was Carlo who had brought all this on himself, and the least he could do would be to work and make amends for his past conduct, as far as lay in his power.

Lidia was about to reply, when the studio door was pushed open abruptly, and Albina showed an excited face in the doorway.

'Contessa Lidia, here is a signore,' she almost gasped, endeavouring to preserve her control. 'He—he wishes to see you. He would not stay downstairs.'

And she drew back, conscious of the bewilderment with which Lidia would receive her visitor, and allowed Mr. Treherne to walk into the room.

Lidia rose hastily, too astonished indeed for words, as the young Englishman came forward and stretched out his hand with a quiet greeting, as though they had been accustomed to meet every day.

'You are welcome, signore,' she said, finding her voice at last, and flushing crimson with shyness, unused as she was to strangers. 'I did not know you were in Florence. You

Padre Antonio rose as they shook hands; he nodded and smiled to the stranger, and then turned to Lidia.

'Good-bye, child; you are engaged now. I will come again before I return to Fiesole this afternoon.'

'It will please me very much,' answered Lidia, following him to the door, where she bade him good-bye.

She came back somewhat timidly to her other visitor, who was examining the picture on the easel.

'My sister and I arrived yesterday,' he said quickly, on perceiving her embarrassment. 'We were very anxious to know how you were, and so I came immediately.'

His tone was much more genial than at their last interview, and less peremptory.

'It was very kind,' said Lidia, a smile lighting up her face. 'Do you like the villa, signore?'

'It is perfect,' replied the young man kindly.

There was a dignity about the little Contessa before which Treherne's usual abruptness faded away. She seemed to demand a certain chivalry in the bare studio, and the poor surroundings did not take away from the dignity of her manner.

'May I look at your picture?' he asked; then added, half smiling, 'I have already done so, without your permission. It is always the same subject—the Madonna.'

'And what better subject could we have, except God Himself?' she asked gravely.

'You might have chosen one less common,' he replied; 'for you paint very well. The peasant's face is life-like.'

'It gave me a great deal of trouble,' said Lidia, smiling.

'And how are you getting on?' he asked.

Yes, she must conquer her shyness and say it—what had been troubling her nearly all the night:

'You did not do as I asked you, signore. You let off part of the debt.'

He frowned.

'You will allow me to be the best judge of my own affairs,' he said. 'I suppose your brother told you. Excuse my abruptness, but I should prefer to let the subject drop.'

tone. It was at this tone that his father had expected the proud little Contessa would take offence. She only flushed a little, and answered quietly:

'Our expenses might be much less than they are, for we still keep the horses——'

'You cannot walk into Florence,' interrupted Treherne. 'Your brother is quite right in keeping them for you. You do not look strong, and driving will do you good.'

She did not reply at once, neither did she think it necessary to say she had never driven in the carriage since they came to Quaracchi.

'Signore, doubtless many would esteem this great kindness on your part,' she said; 'but it is not kind to us. Our mother wished it to be as I wanted to arrange, but you have prevented me from doing so.'

'Contessa Donati,' he replied, 'it is needless for me to repeat that I cannot agree with you on this subject, so with your permission we will not refer to it again,' adding more gently, 'What I want to know is, how you are getting on.'

It was very strange he should be so interested in a girl he had known so short a time, but Treherne's perceptions were quick. Like his father, he had read Carlo's character very easily. Then it must be remembered Lidia had a pretty face, and that went a long way towards enlisting Treherne's sympathies, though they had been already awakened by the fact that she had to live with the most selfish man he had ever known. As he looked down at her now, many little changes in her face and figure told him the burden she bore was no light weight.

'I am very well as I am,' Lidia answered, a slight reserve in her manner. 'I paint a great deal, and my house is in the most beautiful country in the world.'

'Yes, that is true,' said Treherne, going over to the windows and looking out on the olive-clad hills and deep-blue sky.

'It is from there I took the idea of my picture,' she said in a more genial tone, pointing to a shrine below in the high white wall separating the vineyard from the road. 'Beppa, one of the grape-pickers we had last year, sat for me. She has a very beautiful face, and was in great distress at the time because her father would not allow her to marry Luigi. I found her kneeling before the shrine one day, and she made such a pretty picture! Before I had finished the face, the Madonna had heard Beppa's prayer, so that it was difficult for me to make her wear the sad, pleading look: just as it was perfect, she would begin laughing and say how happy she was.'

A half-amused, half-ironical smile spread over Treherne's face.

'So the Madonna heard her prayer,' he said, looking down at the little white shrine. 'Do you think if Beppa had not prayed she would not have got what she wanted?'

'I know what they call the Church of England does not believe in the Madonna,' she said, detecting the scepticism in his tone, 'and it is very strange. You do not pray to the Madonna, signore?'

It was a very grave face, with a pitying expression, that looked up at Treherne.

'No, I do not,' he answered, half smiling at the naïve manner.

'And yet you are very kind, signore,' she said, forgetting her shyness in her wonder; 'it is a great pity. Do you belong to the Church of England?'

'No,' replied Treherne quietly, well aware of the effect his words would have on his listener, yet unable to resist the confession; 'I do not belong to any Church.'

For the moment Lidia did not understand. Then their conversation on the terrace of the Fiesole villa flashed back on her. Was it possible he had been referring to himself when he spoke of the unbeliever? Was she really standing beside one who never prayed to God? He could not see her face; it was turned towards the shrine of the Madonna below in the road.

'You are shocked,' he said at last.

'I am much grieved,' she answered, turning anew to him. 'You have been very kind in coming to see after me. I wish you could enjoy God and the Madonna, for where God is not, there is a great void which nothing can fill. When you look over the vineyards and mountains, is there not a great want in your heart to know who made it all? Does not the air feel empty without God?'

'It was Nature made all,' said Treherne in a bantering tone.

Lidia winced as though she had been hurt.

'It made itself,' she said slowly. 'This is a strange doctrine. To you, signore, there is no God, no heaven, no hell, no sin?'

'There is sin enough in the world; we know that,' said he shortly.

'Then whom do we sin against?' asked Lidia.

'Against the laws of Nature,' he answered. 'Contessa Lidia, I fear you will never understand. You have not seen misery as I have, or perhaps you too would ask, "Where is God?"'

'Go to the churches,' replied Lidia—'I mean our churches—and kneel before the Santissimo; very soon the answer will come to you if you ask. He is there listening to you.'

'It is all very well for those who believe,' he answered; 'but if I went?'

'Oh, signore, do go!' she cried eagerly; 'you have been very kind. It grieves me so much to know you do not believe in God.'

He stood for a moment looking down on her sweet face. Treherne had never come across anyone whose religion was the greater part of her life, whose whole aim was to work in its cause. Lidia was roused out of herself when she spoke of that religion; things unknown to him were heard and seen by her. To Treherne it seemed they might be living in different worlds, so vastly different were their natures and beliefs. She had been quiet and retiring enough before her religion was spoken of; now she seemed to forget he was almost a stranger, and treated him as a friend for whose welfare she was anxious. But although all this passed through his mind, Treherne half smiled at what he considered the flowery imagination of Italians.

'I do not see how it is possible,' went on Lidia, half to herself—'how the world was made; there must have been a beginning. He Who had no beginning, and from Whom existence sprang, must be a God. Who orders all creation? If it orders itself, and we are subject to it, then must we adore the greater Power than ourselves. I must ask Marchese. Perhaps he will understand.'

'Marchese? Who is Marchese?' asked Treherne.

'He is a very good friend of ours,' she answered; 'we have known him a long time. He is clever, and may perhaps be able to explain to you, signore, how very wrong you are!'

Treherne was not accustomed to be told he was wrong, and he felt by no means elated that another should come forward to tell him so.

'Will you paint me a picture?' he asked suddenly.

'Indeed I will, signore!' she replied.

The young man was relieved; their last subject had been dropped. He had never felt more uncertainty in his mind as to whether his doctrine was right than when he met the gaze of those wondering brown eyes. He went on to say that his sister aspired to be a painter, though Treherne smiled as he remembered her poor attempts. In fact, he knew she would be very glad to be taught by the little artist, and when Lidia heard this she was delighted.

'My sister will arrange it all when she comes to see you,' said Treherne.

'She would need a great many lessons before being able to equal her mistress.'

'That is well,' answered Lidia simply; 'if I did not know more than she, I should not be fit to teach her.'

Then Treherne took his leave; his sister would scold him for being late if he did not hurry back.

He paused before the stone shrine of the Madonna as he left the house, and looked through the little iron grating. There was a lighted oil-lamp burning before a picture of the Assumption. The cynical look on Treherne's face passed away. After all, that was a very beautiful religion whose followers honoured and blessed the great God they believed in, and for His sake bore many bitter trials with cheerful patience. Had he not just left one who was an example of this? Her life was no pleasant one, he knew, and yet her nature was not embittered by the crosses sent to her so early in life.

CHAPTER VII.

Carlo returned home late that evening. When Lidia heard him entering the hall she ran down from her studio to greet him. Her brother was in a better humour than when he had left Quaracchi. He answered his sister's welcome quite cordially. She followed him into the drawing-room, but though her heart was beating anxiously she dared ask no questions.

'Oh yes; it is all right,' he said, as he saw her longing to know what had happened. 'Don't ask any questions. I prefer to keep my employment secret.'

And Carlo laughed—not a very pleasant laugh, it is true; but Lidia did not detect the sarcastic ring in it. She was touched by his unselfishness, and went up to him, exclaiming :

'How good you are, Carlo, to sacrifice

everything for me! It must be very hard. Your friends cannot like you the less for your bravery!'

Carlo drew himself away from his sister somewhat abruptly. He did not seem to appreciate her admiration for him, which was very unusual for Carlo. He was particularly silent, too, that evening, and Lydia began to think Marchese Vanutelli had been severe towards this brother, who was so good as to sacrifice his position for her sake. Every now and then she glanced timidly up from her sewing at him, as though longing to ask questions. She tried to imagine she would feel very angry at the idea of working among those who had known her in the days of her prosperity. But strangely and persistently Marchese Vanutelli's words came back to her: 'Would you find it hard if it was to support one you loved?'

The monotony of the evening was relieved by a letter brought in by Albina. Lidia read it with delighted surprise, but Carlo was far from viewing the contents with as much favour as did his sister.

Contessa Mirandoli wrote to say that she

and her husband were returning the very next week to Florence.

They would come and see their dear little Lidia at Quaracchi the day of their arrival.

The Contessa wrote in a whirl of excitement; indeed, Bastiano had had to finish the letter for his wife, as she was quite overcome by the scenes she conjured up, and was prostrate on the sofa. She had been worrying so much lately; her old husband had been ill. This is what Bastiano wrote. Altogether they had had a troublesome time in Switzerland, and were glad enough to return to Florence and make their home near Lidia.

They would arrive any time the following week and surprise her. The Contessa was very fond of giving surprises. Her father declared she married Conte Mirandoli only because her love of startling everyone had prompted her to do so.

Carlo's good-humour vanished when the letter was read, and he showed his disapprobation by replying shortly to all Lidia's delighted exclamations.

Lidia was greatly cheered whenever she thought of the approaching arrival, and it was well she had some distraction, for the days following Carlo's employment at his office were full of perplexity and worry to her.

She did not know where the office was, and Carlo never alluded to his work.

After all, it was very natural he should not like to speak of his humiliation, she thought to herself. Once on asking him if his friends in Florence were the same to him, Carlo had answered evasively; he had only been at the office a few days and there were not many people in Florence now. But what puzzled and distressed Lidia most was that he showed no signs of putting down expenses. The horses used to drive him every morning to Porta San Gallo, one of the gates of Florence, and return for him there in the evening. But she shrank from speaking to him about it, imagining that he had enough to bear already, and so in spite of many bright spots worry came again.

One morning, three or four days after the arrival of the Contessa's letter, Carlo and Marchese Vanutelli were walking slowly up and down on the stone veranda. The Marchese had left Florence very early to come to Quaracchi and see if things were changed. Carlo had met him in the hall, and told him all had been done as he wished. And now they walked on the veranda, Carlo's companion listening gravely to all he had to say.

The request did not seem so easy to make before the Marchese, whose silence disconcerted Carlo. Could it be that their friend saw through his artifices and was too indignant for words? He glanced several times at the face beside him and paused in his speech, as though he wished the rest of his words to be guessed; but the Marchese was listening patiently, and had no idea of interrupting him. And Carlo went on. His salary was very small, as the Marchese had foreseen it would be, and yet he hesitated to give up the horses, for Lidia was fond of driving, and it did her good after painting so much in her studio. Carlo wished to make up to his sister for all he had made her suffer, and—and he came for help to their friend; the debt to the Signor Inglese weighed heavily, too, on his mind. He was very much ashamed to worry the Marchese, but he wished to make amends, and once the Marchese had been kind enough to ask that he (Carlo) should go to him in all his difficulties.

Marchese Vanutelli was silent for some time after the last words were spoken and the hesitating voice ceased. Carlo began to fear he had not hinted his wishes delicately enough since his friend failed to answer him. Many times as they paced the veranda Carlo glanced furtively at the face beside him. But the Marchese never dreamt that selfishness had prompted this appeal to his generosity. He was silent because he thought he had judged Carlo rashly, and he set down the hesitation of Carlo's manner to a very different cause from the real one. Not for a moment did he imagine the young man was acting for his own ends, and that Lidia's comfort was but a secondary affair to him. The Marchese was too noble-hearted himself to suspect others of feelings he did not know or understand. He turned round to Carlo after the pause.

'You have done quite right. I have judged you rashly, Carlo, and you must forgive me. Do not give up the horses; I will look after them. As you say, driving will do Lidia good. It is very kind of you to treat me as your friend.'

Carlo did not answer. He felt strangely uncomfortable. It was not exactly in this way he had expected Marchese Vanutelli to answer his hinted request. Of course it was all the same in the end, but Carlo had not looked for these involuntary rebukes that sounded so bitterly sarcastic to him; indeed, he wondered at first whether the Marchese meant what he said; he did not understand this ignorance of petty feelings, but his companion's next words disarmed these suspicions.

'You will let me be still more of a friend to you, my boy; and, after all, have I not the privileged right of an old friend to help you in all your troubles? You say your salary is small; then, you will allow me to make good the amount you require until you have sufficient for yourself and your sister.'

Yes, it was what Carlo had hinted at, what he had thought to accept without shame; but now the time had come it seemed very different. For one moment Carlo was on the point of making a full confession; the next moment he remembered how disastrous the consequences would be to himself. It was better to keep up the delusion.

'This is very generous of you, Marchese,' he said aloud, in a hesitating, though grave, voice. 'I fear my confidence to you has been merely a begging letter. For myself, you know, I——'

The Marchese raised his hand.

'Say no more,' he interrupted. 'I know very well now no such selfish feeling would prompt your actions. Always treat your sister like this, and I shall be satisfied.'

Carlo winced. He had some honour left that rebelled at this humiliation; but there was ruin staring him in the face if he confessed everything; and, after all, if their friend was so foolishly generous, it was a pity not to take advantage of it. Care for Lidia's comfort was such a good excuse. Carlo glanced at his companion, and wondered if what he once thought of with pleasure was possible. The Marchese certainly interested himself a great deal in their welfare, and Carlo could not understand disinterested kindness.

'Are you going into Florence now?' asked

the Marchese, as they turned to face the length of the veranda again.

Carlo murmured something about it being nearly time; he by no means relished the idea that his companion should follow him into the city.

The Marchese opened his mouth to speak, then checked himself. Carlo had not told him where his office was, but it might remind the young man of a humiliation he had not become accustomed to. Self is not conquered all at once. Better make things easy for Carlo, till he quite understood there was no shame in work.

Carlo, too, looked as if he wanted to speak. He was having a hard struggle within. Honour against self. After all, was it worth the deception?

The Marchese's voice broke the stillness.

'How is your sister, Carlo?' he asked.

'She is working in her studio,' was the reply. 'I am afraid she overtaxes her strength.'

Self had won! The hypocrisy of his own words trampled Carlo's better nature in the dust. The gray olive-trees, with the green vines hanging from branch to branch, together with the marvellously blue sky, was hidden by an ugly cloud from Carlo's eyes. He barely heard the Marchese say he would like to see Lidia's picture.

Almost as he spoke Lidia herself appeared on the veranda. She came swiftly towards them with a merry laugh the Marchese was glad to hear.

'I had only just opened my studio windows,' she exclaimed, 'and I heard your voice, Marchese. How are you to-day?'

She looked from one to the other, as Marchese Vanutelli answered her greeting and asked to see her picture as a favour to an old friend. She slipped her hand in Carlo's arm and stood between the two men.

'It is all right,' she said, glancing proudly up at her brother, who would have been only too glad to get away, though he tried to smile.

'I must be off now, Lidia. I will leave you with the Marchese,' he said.

Almost reluctantly, as though he thought he was doing his friend a wrong, he held out his hand. Marchese Vanutelli grasped it warmly.

'A domani,' he said; 'God bless you, my boy!'

Lidia silently watched her brother disappear. She seemed to have forgotten she was not alone, until she heard her companion's voice.

'Well, child, I am waiting to see your picture.'

'Yes, you must come up now,' she said eagerly; 'there is so much to tell you. Giulia and Bastiano are coming home.'

And she stood back and looked up into his face, sure of finding sympathy in her delight; nor did the Marchese try to hide his pleasure.

'The Contessa will cheer you up,' he said, smiling, as he recalled Giulia Mirandoli's merry face; 'and you want amusement. It is not natural for a child like you to be shut up all day, and I wish you would not paint so much.'

'Oh, I want your opinion on my picture,' she exclaimed. 'And do you know'—she half turned round to him as she led the way upstairs—'the Signor Inglese has returned, and he has seen my picture. He came here the day after he arrived at Fiesole with his sister to ask how we were getting on. Was it not kind of him? But'—and the bright face the Marchese loved so much clouded—' he— he does not believe in God.'

'There are very many so, little one,' he answered, 'in the world, of which you, thank God! know nothing. I am glad they are kind to you. Are they young enough to be your companions?'

'But,' hesitated Lidia, 'if the signore is an atheist, he must not come here.'

They had reached the landing, and Lidia had paused to speak just before the studio door.

'Your faith is strong, child,' he said gravely; 'but there is great danger in holding familiar intercourse with unbelievers, and the strongest faith may be shipwrecked if not carefully guarded. We should, however, pray for such persons, and treat them with courtesy and Christian charity.'

'Yes, you are right, Marchese,' she answered slowly. 'It grieves me very much to know the signore is shut out from God, and I told him I would ask you to explain to him how wrong he was.'

Lidia turned anew to the door and opened it, so she did not see her companion smile. Her heart beat faster as she showed him the picture and waited for his criticism, eagerly scanning his face the while.

'Do you like it, Marchese?' she asked. 'You see, it is our Shrine of the Assumption. Mamma was so fond of that picture.'

'A little Madame Lebrun,' he said with a smile. 'You paint very well, Lidia. I wish you had only to do it for your own amusement.'

'It is very well as it is,' she answered. 'And God is so good; I wonder how anyone can deny Him.'

'May you always wonder,' he said gravely, 'and by that wonder bring souls back to God!'

'If everyone was like you, Marchese, how different the world would be!' she said, looking up at him with the fond respect she had always been accustomed to show him.

'I am glad you should think so, child,' he answered.

A strange tightening round his heart checked further speech. He did not stay very long afterwards, and Lidia followed him downstairs to the little vineyard door.

'Have you still the earring?' she asked, smiling. 'It is to remind you of your own goodness, you know, Marchese.'

'I shall always keep it,' he answered, wondering how he could ever part with her little treasure. 'God bless you! A rivederci!'

'Thank you, Marchese,' she said, her voice quivering. 'You are coming to-morrow, are you not? I heard you say to Carlo, "A domani." You did not say it to me, although I look forward to your visits so much.'

The Marchese roused himself after the short silence that had followed her words. No, it was best not to trouble her yet. She was very young, and love was evidently far from her thoughts. Carlo, too, had turned over a new leaf, and her life would be happier.

Lidia watched him go down the road. He was very good, their Marchese. She thought then no one was like him in the world.

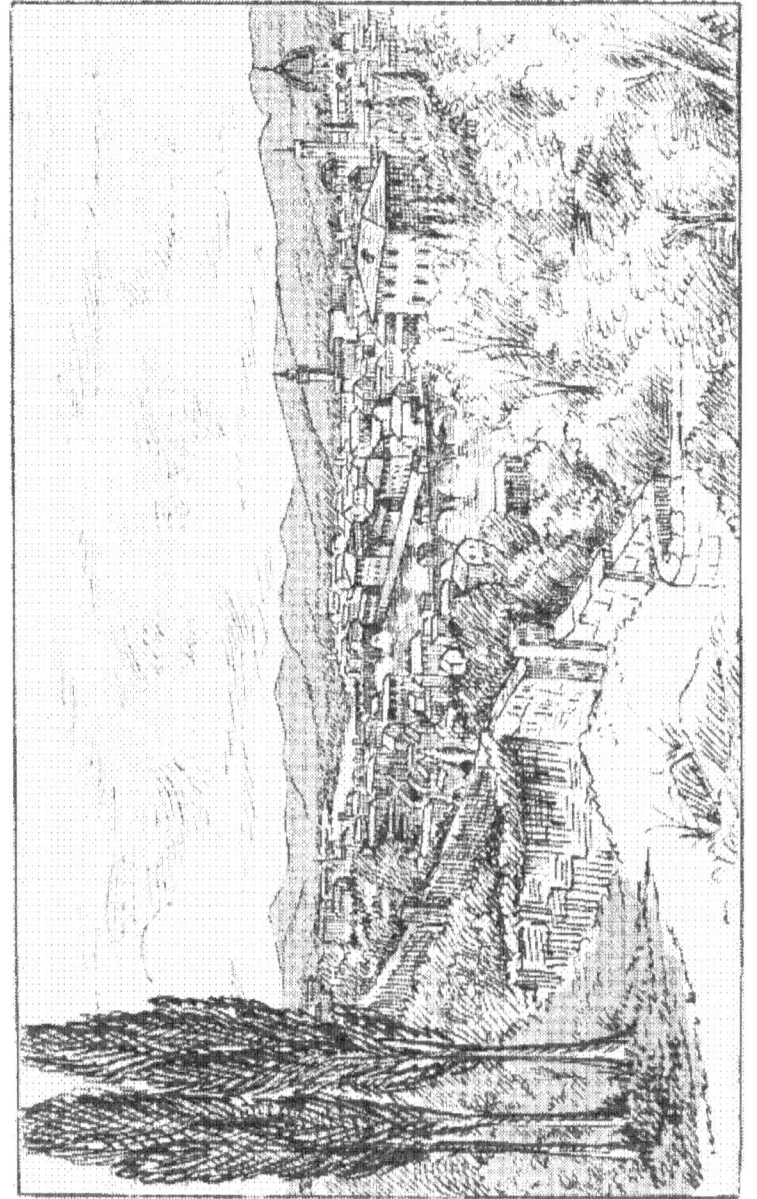

FLORENCE.—*Page* 113.

CHAPTER VIII.

It was evening. The broad and deserted Lung' Arno, with its splendid modern palaces, was bathed in sunshine; so were the quaint Oltr' Arno houses, with their narrow windows and unsafe balconies, on the other side of the swiftly-flowing river. No one knew what a proud aching heart that quiet exterior hid in the Donati's carriage, as it dashed along the Lung' Arno after the suffocating heat of the day, which had driven the inhabitants to the shelter of their cool houses.

Lidia was obeying her brother's wish the day after Marchese Vanutelli's last visit—that she should meet him in the Cascine. The great piazza inside the gates of the Florentine Park was quite deserted; the Viale Delta, with its cool and inviting shade, and the splendid trees entwining their branches far overhead, was an agreeable contrast to the hot dusty square from which it started. It was very still and peaceful underneath the shady trees; here and there some little family party wandered about, enjoying the fresh air of the woods. They glanced curiously up at the lady in her carriage, wondering why she preferred to remain in Florence instead of taking refuge in the mountains, where they themselves longed to go, only the *soldi* were so scarce.

In the stately avenue a fresh breeze blew on Lidia's face, and cooled her after the hot and tiresome drive from Quaracchi. It was not long before she saw Carlo walking slowly down the footpath on one side. She flushed crimson on seeing who was with him. Oh! why had she come out in the carriage that ought not to belong to them? Carlo, turning round by chance, caught sight of his handsome pair of horses. The carriage drew up at his order, and Treherne followed Carlo up to it.

'I am so glad to see you about,' he said, taking her proffered hand, and lifting his hat; 'this splendid air will do you good Would you not like to walk about a little?'

Lidia sprang up. Oh, for anything to drive down the lump in her throat!

A few who were sauntering past under the shady trees turned round to see the young man helping her out; they did not miss the passing expression over Treherne's face as he held for a moment that small gloved hand in his.

'This is gorgeous weather!' he exclaimed; 'some say it is too hot, but I think it perfect.' Then, lowering his voice, so that Carlo, who lingered behind to give his orders to the coachman, should not hear, he said: 'You have been overworking yourself at the Madonna's shrine!'

She looked up, a little surprised at the sudden change in his tone.

'Oh no!' she answered, smiling; 'I have nearly finished it. As soon as I can I will begin yours, signore.'

'Remember, there is no hurry,' he said; 'my sister is coming over to see you. It is not to be a formal call. There is hardly any need for an introduction.'

Again Lidia glanced up at his face, as though she still wondered at the change in his manner—and it was very strange, she thought. How could Miss Treherne know anything about her?

'It is very kind of your sister to trouble about me,' said Lidia; 'and it is a long way from Fiesole to Quaracchi. We might almost see your villa from here, signore.'

Carlo had stayed behind, having met a friend, and left his sister and Treherne to walk on together under the beautiful arbour. Lidia paused in the middle of the avenue to look at the distant Fiesole hill, across the magnificent racecourse just before them, and over the villas, surrounded by their grounds, in the flat country beyond. It was, indeed, a picture that seemed to smile on the gazer. The pink glow of sunset was reflected on the far-off hills. The height of Monte Morello was purple in the misty light. At its base the *loggie* and turrets of magnificent Tuscan villas peeped up between the stately cypresses. So lost, indeed, was Lidia in gazing at this much-loved scene that she hardly heard her companion's words.

'I am coming too,' he said, watching every change on her face, and feeling as though the world had never been so bright as on this day. 'We will have more controversies.'

She turned round.

'No,' she replied quickly, 'I do not like them. They grieve me. It must be so terrible for you to think you will never see those who are dead, and whom you have loved.'

Treherne looked down at her. There was only one life to him. He thought how frail and delicate she seemed, how the blue veins stood out on the white forehead; if she died, they would never meet again. It was his doctrine, and, as she had said, it was a terrible one. In his terror at this awakening he almost lost his self-control; his first impulse was to catch hold of the hand by her side, so close to him, and call on her to live and be strong for his sake. To him there was no hereafter, no future meeting to wait for. Lidia was too engrossed in her thoughts to notice the change in his face, which was but momentary, after all.

When he spoke again his tone was bitter.

'Ah! you are disappointed in me, are you not?'

She was very grave. The setting sun, piercing through the thick foliage, shone on her earnest face.

'Oh, signore,' she exclaimed, in a low voice, 'what pride we must have in ourselves to deny the existence of God!'

At this moment Carlo joined them. For some time the three walked on together, Treherne very silent, while his Italian friend kept up most of the conversation; but at last he roused himself, and turned to Lidia. It was getting late for her to be out; she ought to drive home. Where were the carriages?

He helped her in himself with a strange new gentleness, and spread his own rug over her, in spite of protestations.

'Good-bye; take care of yourself,' he said. 'You look very tired, child.'

She held out her hand to him. The evening light fell softly on her white face and brown eyes; perhaps Treherne held that hand in his longer than was necessary.

'It is very late,' he said; 'I forgot you in my selfish pleasure. The carriage ought to be closed. Donati.'

'Ah, true! I suppose it would be better,' replied Carlo.

Lidia sank back, feeling as though she would rather be on the hard wooden chairs at Quaracchi.

Treherne did not see the gaily-lighted streets when he drove home, or the life that had suddenly awakened in them after the day's heat. His ears, too, were deaf to the *cicade's* song on the winding road up to the Fiesole villa.

There was another whose thoughts were full of 'child.'

* * * * *

It was a very warm day. Albina had come up to tell this to Lidia, who was painting in her studio. She lingered awhile, after imparting the news, to admire a few little sketches pinned about on the walls. It was certainly very hot. Even the irrepressible *cicade* seemed to have had all their impudence taken from them by the heat, and only a faint chirrup in the olive-trees now and then announced to the world they were still alive. The air was perfectly still; the very country seemed to have closed its eyes in peaceful sleep; so that, when a sudden peal of merry laughter broke the silence, Lidia started to her feet, and looked wonderingly at Albina, who turned from contemplating her mistress's works of art, and exclaimed: 'Madonna Santa! whoever is that?' in a somewhat irritated tone of voice, as if she could not understand how anyone could exert themselves to laugh on a day like this.

But when the first surprise was over, and footsteps told them someone was entering the house by the veranda, Lidia knew very well who it was. She threw down her palette and brush, hardly taking heed of where they fell, and ran to the door that Albina had already opened.

In the passage outside stood a little lady, who was evidently the author of the laugh that had so startled the summer air; for her brown eyes were dancing with delight, and her face flushed with excitement. A little behind her was a gentleman, whose amused smile had not died away when Albina opened the door. He it was who called to Lidia, as she stood in the doorway:

'Here we are at last! Do you not recognise us?'

And then Lidia was in her cousin's arms, while Albina stood by gesticulating wildly, and at a loss to find suitable words in her excitement.

'Oh, carina mia, I am so glad to see you again!' cried Contessa Mirandoli; 'it seemed as though we should never come back to Florence, and I wanted to comfort you, piccina; the loss was also mine.'

And the dancing brown eyes grew soft and tender as they fell on Lidia's quivering face.

'Now go to Bastiano,' she said; 'Bastiano and I thought the train would never arrive. How are you, Albina? Ah, I need not ask!'

'No, indeed, grazia de cielo!' answered Albina; 'but it is far from right with the Contessina.'

'No; you do not look well, Lidia,' said Conte Mirandoli, as he greeted her.

'Oh, nonsense!' exclaimed the young girl, laughing. 'Come in here and sit down. How tired you must be!—Albina, go and get some wine for the travellers.'

She led the way into the studio, and made her welcome visitors sit down and rest. Standing up before them, she was able to see if there were any changes in the faces she loved so much. Contessa Mirandoli was as well as ever, but her husband looked worn and thin, as though he had indeed passed through a severe illness.

'Oh yes; it was a dreadful time!' exclaimed the Contessa, clasping her hands as she noticed Lidia's scrutiny. 'Every day Bastiano got thinner and thinner; I thought he was going to disappear altogether.'

'She used to sit and look at me,' added Conte Mirandoli, laughing, 'as though expecting me to fade away every moment; and she wished to print my features on her memory before I utterly disappeared, but you see I am all right now. It is of you, piccina, we want to hear, and how are you getting on?'

'You know everything changed very much after she—she died,' answered Lidia, turning from one to the other. 'We are not so rich now as we were; the Fiesole villa does not belong to us any more.'

'Not belong to you any more!' repeated the Contessa. 'You never said a word of this in your letters; they were always so cheerful!'

'There was no good talking about it,' said Lidia, going up to her cousin, and kneeling down beside her; 'and you had enough to distress you without my adding to your trouble. And now it is all right, I hope. Carlo has his work every day in Florence; he is there now.'

'Tell us all about it,' said the Contessa quickly.

And Lidia did so — the whole account of their life since her mother died. Try as she did to make it otherwise, the blame could not but fall on Carlo. Conte Mirandoli was frowning when the story was over, and even his wife's merry face was severe.

'You should have told me of this,' exclaimed the Contessa. 'We had no idea things had so changed. We thought you had only come for rest to Quaracchi. It was unkind of you to keep it from us.'

'But Carlo is working to make it all right,' said Conte Mirandoli cheerfully, as he saw Lidia's wistful face.

'Yes; the Marchese arranged it all,' she said, with a contented sigh.

'There is no one like that man,' said the Contessa decidedly. 'And about those English people, piccina: you say they are kind to you?'

'Oh, very kind!' replied Lidia. 'You will see them this afternoon; the signorina wrote and told me she was coming. I have never seen her yet.'

'How delightful!' exclaimed the Contessa. —'Ah, figlia mia!' she added to Albina, who entered with the refreshments; 'we have all had a distressing time.'

Ah, yes; the Contessina had told Albina the Signor Conte had been ill. He was very well now, was he not?

Albina scrutinized his face. They also had had a hard time; the Contessina did nothing but work at her picture all day, and Marchese Vanutelli disapproved of it—he had said so only the other day to her (Albina). But, oh! the Contessina would have her way.

'That is very wrong of you, Lidia,' said her cousin, as she took the glass of wine; 'now Carlo works there is no need for you to do so. I suppose that is your picture on the easel? No! I shall not look at it; I am too angry.'

'It is one the Signor Inglese ordered,' said Lidia, smiling. 'You are very severe on me, Giulia.'

'Tell us more of this English family,' said the Conte, settling himself comfortably in his chair. 'Are they elderly people?'

'Oh no!' answered Albina; 'the signore is quite young. It is true I have not seen the signorina; but I do not doubt she is young, too.'

'You will see them this afternoon,' said Lidia, sitting down at last to take a rest. 'Indeed, they said in the note they would come about this time.'

And just as she spoke there was a ring at the bell below. Albina vanished. The Contessa started up excitedly.

'There they are!' she exclaimed. 'Bastiano, am I tidy? Do I look as if I had come from Switzerland? Mio bimbo, your tie is crooked!'

She went up to her husband and settled the tie to her satisfaction.

'Nothing gives a man so ruffled an appearance as a crooked tie,' she continued for Lidia's benefit, as the Conte, with a laugh, kissed his wife's hands. 'Never allow your husband to have a crooked tie, Lidia, otherwise his appearance is ruined, in spite of fine clothes. And now, my dear, perhaps you had better go down and receive your guests.'

'Oh, you will come, too?' implored Lidia, turning to them both.

'Oh yes; of course,' replied the Contessa. 'Bastiano and I will follow you.'

Her visitors were on the veranda. Albina came up and told Lidia, who went downstairs, followed by the Conte and his wife. The brother and sister were looking out on the vineyard before them when Lidia appeared. The sun had gone round to the other side of the old farmhouse, a slight breeze had sprung up and stirred through the olive-trees, rousing the busy insect life. Treherne was the first to hear her step, and turned round. His sister, though much older than he was, looked younger; she had a quantity of fair curly hair, and Lidia thought the merry blue eyes were beautiful, and admired the English girl's fairness, as all Italians do.

Miss Treherne held out her hand with such a cordial greeting that Lidia's shyness faded away.

'I am so glad to see you at last!' she exclaimed; 'and I have heard so much of you and beautiful Quaracchi.'

She did not notice Contessa Mirandoli in the room behind them, so she did not see the little lady's significant smile as her eyes rested approvingly on the young Englishman, who was waiting to greet her cousin with an expression in his eyes the Contessa had so often seen in someone else's.

She did not remain long in retirement, but came forward with her husband to be presented by Lidia. She greeted the brother and sister like old friends; she regretted so much not being able to speak English, she only knew French, but her husband would interpret what she could not make clear to them.

It did not take long for them all to be laughing and chatting on the veranda as though they had seen each other many a time before. Now and then the Contessa, watching Treherne's face, saw him look at her cousin with the half-proud, half-tender light in his eyes she had already noticed, but he seldom addressed Lidia; indeed, the Contessa's troubles were the engrossing subject of conversation.

'When once Giulia has begun to talk of Switzerland,' said her husband, laughing, 'she will never stop.'

'Let us hear your experiences, Contessa; may we?' asked Treherne.

'My experiences!' And the little Italian lady threw up her hands. 'I tremble to think of them. When we first arrived in Switzerland it was all very well. We went into an hotel; but when I commenced housekeeping in Berne—Santa Vergine!—my troubles began. I did not know any German; I depended entirely on my husband, and when he got ill —oh, it was terrible! No; I shall never, never go back there again. You know we went up to Zermatt after my husband got better. It was a dreadful expense,' added the Contessa, with charming candour, 'and prevented us from coming to Florence as soon as we wanted to. But the doctor ordered change for Bastiano. O Dio mio! What I endured in that journey! We drove from

Visp to St. Nicholas, where we passed the night; then up the next morning and on to Zermatt. My husband had bought a conversation-book in four languages at Geneva before we started, and with this we felt bold enough to attack a vetturino in German. We asked how far it was to St. Nicholas, and how long it would take to drive there. The man's answers were also given in this delightful little book. Bastiano had learnt the questions, and I knew the answers by heart. Well, the vetturino commenced a long sentence I could not understand a bit, but I thought all the time perhaps the stupid fellow was leading up to the answer in the book; he was not, though, and goodness knows what he did say. We asked him a few more questions to give him another chance, but it was useless, and I do not know what we should have done had not an Englishman come forward and helped us. I tried the vetturino with a few more pretty questions as we climbed up the hill. Once I thought he was giving me the answers in the book, and I wanted to say "Go slower," but I did not know what "Go slower" was in German, and Bastiano told me to stop such a one-sided conversation, or the people in the carriage behind us would think we were escaped lunatics. Yes; Bastiano can be very rude when he likes, and the petting he had had when he was ill made him impertinent.'

'You liked Zermatt, though,' said Treherne, after the merriment caused by the Contessa's story of her troubles had ceased.

'That is what everyone said to me,' she replied, with an injured air. 'Now, Bastiano used to sit and be content to look at the Matterhorn for hours. He said it was so beautiful. But I—I did not care for such things. The mountains shut out the view so.'

Miss Treherne laughed merrily.

'But the mountains are what everyone goes to see in Switzerland,' she said.

'So they tell me,' replied the Contessa. 'For my part, I much prefer a plain like the Val d'Arno, where you can see about you, and the mountains are in the distance. I do not like being shut in by big lumps of earth that people are for ever climbing and breaking their necks over. I cannot understand it. Bastiano drove me to the verge of my grave for a week by wanting to climb the Matterhorn, and one of the guides said to me: "It is quite safe, madame. We are all tied together, and are able to save each other. The most dangerous part is at the shoulder, where we have to climb on our hands and knees with"—I don't know how many thousand feet he said—"above and below us." I thanked him for trying to reassure me. That night I packed up all our things and ordered the carriage to take us down to Visp as early as possible the next morning, and Bastiano and I left Zermatt.'

'Then you will not go back again?' said Lidia, smiling. 'You will stay with us, Giulia.'

'Indeed, yes. I would rather endure this heat,' replied the Contessa, 'than go in those parts again. But I am talking too much of myself. Tell me of the people in Florence.' And the lively little lady rattled off all she wanted to know about her friends. How was Count Cafferecci. She owed him a grudge; it was he who had advised Bastiano and herself to economize in Switzerland. And the Count Bastianelli? The last time she had seen him he was suffering from a fall from his horse, poveretto! So sad; it made his face look more comical than ever. And had the Count Malvezzi's horse won at the Florentine races? Oh, she was very sorry it had! She did not like sallow-faced young men with black beards. It might be prejudice, but they always reminded her of brigands and knives. Had Signora Mascardi returned? Had the Marchesa di Villalosa married the little Russian in the yellow overcoat? Had the Contessa Leonadi succeeded in marrying her hideous daughter? Ah! she would spare her husband's feelings. She knew he was devoted to the Contessina Matilde. And Marchese Vanutelli? Their dear Marchese! Was he as good and kind as ever? Ah! she was silly to ask that question. Their friend would never change.

She stopped, out of breath at last, and asked someone to answer all her questions. As this was quite impossible, Treherne ventured one. Who was Marchese Vanutelli? He had heard so much of him in Florence, and would like to know such a popular man.

'Oh, everyone loves him!' exclaimed the

Contessa. 'He is so good, and a very old, old friend of ours. I wish he would come now we are all together.'

'He was here a few days ago,' said Lidia. 'He knows you are coming, Giulia.'

'In that case I am surprised he does not call every day on the chance of seeing me,' remarked the Contessa.

And then Miss Treherne suddenly remembered Lidia's picture that she wanted so much to see—the 'Madonna's Shrine,' which her brother had admired.

Lidia hesitated. Treherne noticed the hesitation immediately, and guessed what had become of the painting.

'Maisy must wait till my picture is finished,' he said quickly.

Oh, if Lidia had begun her brother's picture, Miss Treherne would so like to see it! She was passionately fond of painting, and it was this love for art that made the English girl and the little Italian Contessa such friends. She had only sketched it, Lidia said, as she rose to show the way. But Miss Treherne was eager to see it, and so they left the other three laughing and talking on the veranda.

'Well, I think you were right in hinting I should not know what it is,' said Miss Treherne, after examining the picture on the easel. 'I see there is a wayside cross and a figure kneeling. Is there not someone in the foreground?'

Lidia nodded.

'Well,' said her friend slowly, 'I wish you had chosen some other subject. You do not mind me saying so, do you?'

'Oh no, no!' replied Lidia.

'Because,' hesitated Miss Treherne, 'my brother is not—not a religious man, and he might have preferred something else.'

'He said I might choose what subject I liked,' replied Lidia, looking a little anxiously at her companion. 'If he does not like it I will paint another.'

'You are not offended, I hope, Contessa?' asked Miss Treherne. 'And you don't mind me calling you Contessa, do you? Contessa Lidia is so formal.'

'Call me what you like,' answered Lidia, smiling. 'I am not offended; why should I be?'

'Oh, some people do not like being told

what to do!' said Miss Treherne decidedly. 'They think if they are huffy they look better, I suppose. I thought you did not know about my brother. Is it not a shameful doctrine?'

'It is a dreadful one,' replied Lidia. 'Every time I look out on the olives and vineyards I wonder how anyone can live and say there is no God.'

'Then you are extra good, you know,' said Miss Treherne. 'Frank told me so; he said it was all there without pomp or show.'

'That is just what you always say of us,' answered Lidia, with a puzzled air, 'that we have so much ceremony, so little at the bottom. Rosa, the English girl at the convent with me, used to say the same. But I put it to you, signorina, when we are serving some great king, is there not much ceremony to receive him and to honour him? How much more we must use in the presence of God!'

'Still, there is a great deal of useless pomp in your Church,' said Miss Treherne. 'Forgive my candour.'

Lidia smiled.

'But, signorina,' she answered, 'take a poor

contadina out of a very desolate part of the country, who had seen nothing of the world, and was suddenly brought to the court of some great king, would she not think all the splendid entertainments useless? You know we do not turn our backs on royalty. I take that as a little example. The contadina wonders why all walk in such a strange fashion, why they cannot turn round and go out as she would do. As the contadina judges, so do you when you come to our churches.'

'You are right,' said Miss Treherne frankly. 'I dare say we do judge without sufficient knowledge. Some of our remarks must amuse you very much.'

'Yes,' replied Lidia, smiling a little, 'when I read in some English books that the priests say Mass in the evening, and recite the Gloria over a death-bed.'

Miss Treherne laughed. She knew enough of Catholics to understand the absurdity of these mistakes.

'Well, and your other picture, Contessa?' she said, looking round—'the "Madonna's Shrine." Frank said it was beautiful.'

'I have sold it,' replied Lidia. 'We are

not well off, as you know. If you would like to see it, it is in Bertoldi's shop in the Via dei Fossi.'

'I will go there,' said Miss Treherne. 'And now, Contessa, you must give me lessons. My brother told me he spoke to you about them. I will come to you. I love driving. I leave you to name the days and what you will take for the lessons. Frank says you paint beautifully, and he is a good judge.'

'Any day you choose to fix,' answered Lidia quietly. 'What I will take for the lessons will be the pleasure of being with you.'

'Oh dear no!' replied Miss Treherne. 'I could not think of such a thing. We will have them three times a week, at ten francs a lesson.'

'No,' said Lidia firmly; 'I cannot, signorina. You know our position with regard to your father. How could I accept money from you while we are still in your debt?'

It was useless for her friend to urge how absurd this was; that, had she not met Lidia, she would have taken and paid for lessons of someone else. Miss Treherne declared she had nothing to do with what they owed her father. But Lidia did not understand that; she preferred to do it for pleasure. Then Miss Treherne wanted to value her lessons at ten francs, and in this way Lidia could pay the debt that was weighing so on her mind.

'You are very kind and good,' faltered Lidia; 'but the arrangement—— I would rather not.'

'Oh, Contessa, what a proud little girl you are!' exclaimed Miss Treherne. 'Why not agree to my proposal?'

'Am I very proud?' said Lidia. 'Oh, signorina! it is on account of my mother. She wished it to be arranged that we should pay. Let me give you the lessons; it will be a great pleasure to me.'

'But I shall interrupt your painting,' said Miss Treherne uneasily.

'Oh no,' replied Lidia. 'I shall find time to paint, and we will do it together. It will be very pleasant.'

Miss Treherne looked down into the Italian girl's face. 'Ah!' she thought, 'no wonder Frank thinks Quaracchi so beautiful.' She bent and kissed Lidia.

'Then we will arrange it so, child,' she said kindly. 'Shall we have Monday, Wednesday and Saturday?'

'Yes,' answered Lidia; 'I am satisfied.'

Below, under the veranda, the group of three was a merry one; indeed, how could they help laughing at the Contessa's droll descriptions of their life in Switzerland, that she seemed never tired of talking about and depreciating?

A very quiet 'Contessa Mirandoli!' made the little lady start to her feet.

Marchese Vanutelli was standing behind her, smiling, and with outstretched hand. While they were making merry, he had come unseen on the veranda.

'You do not mean to say my wish has been answered!' she exclaimed breathlessly, and holding out both her hands, while her husband and Treherne rose also. 'I have been longing for you to come!' she cried. 'Bastiano, does it not seem a miracle?'

'I came to see if you had arrived,' said the Marchese, as he shook hands with Conte Mirandoli, and glanced at that other figure standing apart from them, facing the vineyard.

'Lidia told me she expected you at any moment. I am very glad to welcome you back to Florence. You have been so long away.'

'It has seemed a century!' exclaimed the Contessa. 'I am sure we are delighted to be back, though we found dreadful changes.'

'Yes, indeed,' said the Marchese gravely. 'Lidia told me you were ill,' turning to the Conte; 'but you are all right now, I hope. Florence will suit you better than any other place, and we must try and get you well.'

'That is what my wife has told me ever since we left it,' said Conte Mirandoli. 'I must say the year's absence was no pleasant one.'

'You must let me present Signor Trerni to you,' cried the Contessa, laying her hand on the Marchese's arm. 'Signore!' She beckoned to Treherne. 'You, too, wanted the Marchese to come, that you might make the acquaintance of the most popular man in Florence.'

Treherne came forward. Like everyone else—old, young, rich, and poor—he felt the charm of the noble face. It was no ordinary face, whose owner Treherne could have trusted at first sight.

The Marchese, too, was favourably impressed. Lidia had said these English friends of hers were very kind to them, and he held out his hand with a cordiality he seldom showed towards strangers.

'This is a very welcome meeting,' he said; then added courteously, 'I had no idea my fame reached to Fiesole; but I have heard of you, signore, and I am pleased to be able at last to thank you for your kindness to my friends.'

There was nothing to thank him for, Treherne answered quickly; and the Marchese looked round as though in search of the friends he spoke of.

'We were entertaining ourselves,' said the Contessa. 'Carlo is in Florence. Lidia is showing her picture to Signorina Trerni. I will call her.'

She ran down the veranda steps and called her cousin underneath the studio window.

'I am glad to see Florence is not quite deserted,' said the Marchese to Treherne. 'Everyone has run away from the heat, and you, too, Conte, have appeared just at the right time to cheer our solitude.'

'Yes; my wife would insist upon returning,' replied Conte Mirandoli; 'and I am sure, in spite of the heat, I am not sorry to be back.'

A moment after Lidia followed Miss Treherne on to the veranda. She greeted the Marchese delightedly.

'Just what Giulia and all of us were hoping!' she exclaimed. 'This has been a lovely day.'

In a very short time they were talking as merrily as ever with the new guest. The Contessa aired all her grievances again before this new sympathizer. The bright colour had come back into Lidia's face, and her laugh was as gay as the rest. Marchese Vanutelli was glad to hear it. He watched the change with pleasure. She was happy now; perhaps soon the day would come when he could tell her how much he loved her and wished to take care of her all his life. Many scenes came up before the Marchese's eyes even while the laughter echoed in the veranda. He began to wonder how he could make his home more cheerful for her, how he could make amends for all she had borne during the past sad months. And he would have his wife to welcome him home. He would ask for nothing more except to make her happy. The Contessa's voice drove the pictures away.

'Well, Marchese, have you any news?'

'Of course!' he exclaimed, suddenly recollecting himself. 'I was forgetting one of the reasons that brought me to Quaracchi. The Palazzo Vecchio is to be illuminated the day after to-morrow; it has just been decided on in honour of our new mayor. Lidia was always so fond of going to see it, and perhaps you, Contessa, will not disdain to notice it after your absence.'

No, indeed, the Contessa was delighted. It was true she used to ignore the sight, saying it was only for the people; but she had discarded that foolish idea now. Had their English friends seen it? Ah! but they should go. It was beautiful. Lidia heard the news with pleasure, too, then with a little pain. The last time the Palazzo Vecchio was illuminated she had witnessed the lovely sight with her mother. The Marchese, as he listened to the Contessa's exclamations, caught sight of the grave face.

'Would you not like to go?' he asked.

She looked up quickly.

'Oh yes, very much; only—you remember, Marchese, do you not?'

'Yes, child,' he answered; 'and I do not wish you to forget the past, but not to think of it too much.'

Then Miss Treherne made a suggestion. Why could they not all come up to Fiesole and have dinner with them, after which they could drive down to the Piazza della Signoria and witness the fête? Oh yes; they must all come! Lidia's brother also; it would be so pleasant!

'This is very kind of you,' said the Contessa gratefully, half turning towards Lidia, who drew back a little; she was so unaccustomed to going out.

Treherne came forward.

'You will not refuse!' he exclaimed eagerly.

The Marchese looked up at him, standing before Lidia, and his eyes were opened when he saw the young man's face. Just for the moment a mist hid the group from Marchese Vanutelli's eyes, but he was himself again immediately.

'You will accept the signorina's kind invitation, bimba,' he said gravely, seeing Treherne's eagerness, and knowing very well she would act by his advice; and Miss Treherne smiled a little as she saw Lidia's entire confidence in him expressed in so many ways.

'Then you, Marchese,' said Treherne, turning to him after Lidia had tendered her grateful thanks, and the Conte and his wife expressed themselves delighted at the idea.

Marchese Vanutelli smiled.

'It is most kind of you to think of me, signore,' he answered; 'but my business keeps me all day in Florence. Perhaps I shall be able to join you in the piazza.'

'I am very sorry you will not come to us,' said Miss Treherne, with true regret. She, like her brother, was attracted by the grave, kind face that bore witness of the noble nature within.

Twilight crept on as they sat under the veranda; the fireflies were lighting up the dusky olive-groves before them, the bats had taken the place of chirping swallows and noisy *cicale*. At last Miss Treherne declared they ought to be off; they had trespassed on the Contessa's hospitality for so long.

'Our staying has enabled us to meet you, though, signore,' said Treherne, as they all stood together in the road bidding each other good-bye, and he held out his hand to Marchese Vanutelli.

Very little of the world-wise Treherne seemed left. Lidia was there and the Marchese, and somehow before these two his disbelief in human goodness faded away. Though he did not know why, he was unable to say that honour was dead when the Marchese grasped his hand warmly and bade him good-night; and when he turned to Lidia and held her hand, a sudden doubt as to whether his whole life had not been a mistake overpowered him. A cool breeze was blowing down the country road; the little white shrine in the wall beside them looked ghostly in the waning light.

'I wonder,' something made Treherne say to her as they stood a little apart from the rest, 'if you ever pray for those who do not believe.'

'I pray for you, signore,' she answered gravely, 'ever since you told me.'

Marchese Vanutelli left at the same time as the Trehernes' carriage vanished out of sight.

'You are looking quite merry,' he said before leaving, as he held the hand so dear to him, and saw Lidia's dancing brown eyes. 'Contessa Mirandoli,' he turned half smiling to that little lady, 'I leave her in your charge; it is you who have worked the change.'

'I wish you were coming up to the villa with us,' said Lidia; 'but you will be on the piazza, will you not? Good-bye, Marchese.'

CHAPTER IX.

CARLO returned home very soon after Marchese Vanutelli's departure. His face fell considerably when Albina met him in the hall and told him of the Conte and Contessa Mirandoli's arrival, and their intention to stay at Quaracchi for the night. He by no means relished the idea of the Contessa settling in Florence; his cousin was not fond of keeping her affairs to herself, and who knows but what she might be equally communicative about his? He tried to greet her cordially on entering the *salone*, but there was a certain restraint in his manner which the sharp little Contessa noticed immediately.

'Bastiano,' she said that night to her husband, when they had retired, 'I would not trust that boy with a soldo. How can brother and sister be so unlike?'

'Well, and you won't tell me?'

It was the Contessa who spoke the next morning to Carlo as the two stood in the hall of the Quaracchi home. She was looking up at her cousin with a disdainful smile, which Carlo did not like at all. It was not quite so easy to deceive Giulia about the true state of their affairs, as it was the more confiding Lidia. The Contessa wanted to know all about his work. What did he do at his office, and how much salary did he get? She was not timid of hurting his feelings, she had often declared Carlo had none at all; she always held her cousin in very small respect, and that was why Carlo had not looked forward to her arrival. He frowned at the question, repeated several times that morning.

'Because I prefer to be silent about it,' he answered.

'How rude you are, and what a face to put on!' exclaimed the Contessa saucily. 'Where is this wonderful office of yours that pays you so well that you can keep your carriage and pair?'

And she glanced through the open hall-door to where the horses stood in the road, ready to drive their master into Florence. Carlo did not answer, only looked blacker than ever; he thought to put a stop to this unwelcome conversation by leaving his cousin with a curt, 'Good-bye!' but she was not so easily put aside.

'Oh, wait a bit!' she said, laughing. 'Cannot Bastiano get a clerkship in this generous firm?'

Carlo stopped. Perhaps it would be better to tell her how he was able to have the horses. It might silence her, and she would not be likely to tell Lidia. So he turned round again.

'Marchese Vanutelli wished me to keep them for Lidia,' he answered in a low voice. 'He arranges about it all.'

It was well that Carlo, wrapt up in himself, did not notice the expression on his cousin's face.

'Ah!' she exclaimed. 'So you like to give the poor things a little exercise to the Porta San Gallo every morning. You are quite right. They would not get much outing otherwise.'

The Contessa smiled a very sarcastic smile

for such a good-natured little person. Carlo changed colour.

'You do not believe me!' he said sharply. 'You can go and ask Vanutelli——'

'Oh, I believe *that!*' she answered. 'What I do not believe is—this story about an office.' She stood back and looked defiantly up at her tall, handsome cousin.

Carlo's face became quite gray. For a moment he stood looking down at the Contessa with an expression in his eyes that even that dauntless little lady was very nearly being afraid of. Then he brushed past her and went out to his carriage in the road.

'Poor Lidia!' she exclaimed half to herself. 'It is just what I thought!'

She and her husband went to Florence that morning to look out for a suitable house. They promised to return to Quaracchi in the evening if their search was fruitless. Before they left the Contessa had spoken very seriously to Lidia about her brother, and now Lidia, seated before her easel, was unable to work, so absorbed was she in this new and dreadful suspicion. No, it could not be that Carlo had been deceiving them all the while.

If he had not been working, where could the money have come from that he professed to have earned at the office? For the Contessa had refrained from mentioning what Marchese Vanutelli had done. No, it was impossible! It must be impossible! But she could not work, and Albina failed to cheer her up. And at last, unable to be still any longer, Lidia decided to go into Florence to see if her picture of the 'Madonna's Shrine' had been bought.

The steam-tram was just starting, and, sinking down in a corner, she leant her aching head back wearily and watched the vineyards and olive-groves fly past her. Tears did not come now so easily as they used to, and Lidia's eyes were hot and dry. Only yesterday all had seemed so bright and happy. How she had laboured and tried to act for the best, and it was all in vain. How she despised the deception, if it was as Contessa Mirandoli had said, and all those petty lies were told and acted.

'O Dio mio! it may not be!' she exclaimed, clasping her hands. 'And even so it is not my place to condemn. Did not mamma say the very same, and she was better than I?'

A hot sirocco was blowing down the deserted streets, where Lidia took refuge in the shade. She was bound for Bertoldi's shop, where good news awaited her.

Signor Bertoldi had never seen the Contessa Lidia Donati. He did not know that the pale-faced lady was the sister of the Marchese Donati, who drove the best horses in Florence. He came forward—a little, bustling man—expecting some order, and was somewhat surprised when he learnt that the painter of the 'Madonna's Shrine,' which had taken his artistic fancies by storm, now stood before him. It was already sold at an immense price, he told Lidia, only half an hour before she entered the shop. Indeed, he got more than he had asked for it, so that he felt in duty bound to give the signora more money for the picture. This was very unexpected. Lidia asked with bated breath who was the munificent buyer! Bertoldi shrugged his shoulders and said, 'Chi lo sa?' (Who knows?). He counted out the money on a little table. Lidia wondered if he would ever stop.

'Oh, signore,' she exclaimed, 'what a lot you must have had for the picture!'

'Here it is!' said the little man, almost as delighted at her unexpected good fortune as she was herself. 'It was marvellous. Your pictures will sell well, signora. Paint another and send it to me. You may name your own price.'

Lidia tightly clasped her purse with the wonderful wealth inside. And then she walked to the Barriera delle Cure, where the steam-tram started for San Dominica, and from there she intended to ascend the Fiesole hill. Lidia hardly felt the hot wind blowing in her face, and she forgot to feel tired, so intent was she on reaching Fiesole. And when she alighted from the dusty tram and walked slowly up the steep road a strange mist was before her eyes that almost blotted out the campanile of the Fiesole church above her, and the large Franciscan convent that crowned the hill. From the avenue of her old home she caught a glimpse of the city below and San Miniato, whose gold mosaic was glittering in the sunshine. But there was no time to indulge in vain regrets. God had ordered her life as He thought best, and Lidia bowed her head as she walked between the dark cypresses. 'His Will be done!'

Both master and mistress were out, but the signora was asked to come in and wait for them. But Lidia had no time, and wrote a hurried little note as she stood in the familiar hall, begging Mr. Treherne to take the money she left, as she was perfectly able to give it.

It was late when Lidia returned home, half fainting with fatigue, and somewhat remorseful at having had to engage a cab at Porta San Gallo to drive her home; but she was able to pay for it out of her earnings, which was a relief. Yes; the Signor Marchese had returned earlier than usual that afternoon, Albina told her young mistress when she entered the hall. He was in the *salone*, and something must have annoyed him, for he was very much out of temper. The Contessina was looking tired. Would she not rest a little and take some wine before going to see her brother? Lidia shook her head. Albina watched her mistress pause before the room where Carlo was sitting, and the hand stretched out to open the door shook perceptibly; but Lidia controlled her anxiety in a moment and entered. The windows were open; Carlo had drawn his chair half on to the veranda, and was reading his paper. He looked up on hearing someone come in. The expression on his sister's face silenced the impatient words with which he was going to greet her. He watched her come towards him and saw her hesitation before she spoke.

'Carlo'—the voice sounded very strange and far away—'Giulia told me this morning she did not believe you had any employment in Florence. Is she right?'

Carlo started up. Angry though he was, he could not find fault with the words so quietly spoken or declare they were unjust. He made a step towards the veranda, but Lidia's hand detained him.

'Carlo,' she said, in the same monotonous voice, 'tell me the truth.'

For a moment the brother looked sullenly down at the small figure by his side, the determination to know everything so plainly written on her face.

Then it all came out. Carlo told the tale

defiantly. He had never wanted to work. If he had deceived her, it was all her fault; she forced it on him. Did she think he spent a pleasant time away from Quaracchi every day? Carlo laughed sarcastically. It was true he had still a good many of his friends who had not left Florence, but many a time he had been on the point of returning home during the day; it was often so dull for him waiting till he could return. Yes; he would tell her everything. She was always talking of the expensive horses; well, Vanutelli kept them for her. Carlo had told him his sister was fond of driving, and the money she thought was his salary came also from their friend. All the miserable plotting to benefit himself was laid bare.

It was her fault, he ended; she should not have forced the deception on him.

A dead silence followed his words. Carlo stood with his back to Lidia, angry, rebellious thoughts filling his head. He wondered with reckless despair what would happen now. For some time he waited for the bitter reproaches to come. He half turned round. Lidia stood immovable behind him, with a face like ashes; her very lips were colourless, and the hands on the back of a chair were trembling convulsively. She seemed to be looking past her brother at something that was even beyond the vineyard. Frightened though he was at her emotion, it awed him so much that he could not move or speak.

'Carlo,' she said, very quietly, still not moving, 'Marchese Vanutelli must know of this.'

No reproach came; only Lidia, seeing he was silent, repeated her words. Carlo faced the vineyard again, a sullen look on his face.

'It is not your deceiving me I mind,' said Lidia, still preserving her calm, as though fearing to lose her control if she gave signs of any outward emotion. 'It is—this deception to—our friend, who has been so—good—so faithful to us—in all our bitter trials.'

She spoke in short pauses, as though forgetting the language she used.

'You must tell him all this.'

'I shall not,' was the muttered reply.

Lidia's face quivered. Once more she had to battle down all the scorn she felt for her brother's cowardice.

'Marchese must know,' she said; 'either you or I must tell him.'

There was no answer.

'Carlo, look round at me,' she said. 'Am I to tell Marchese?'

'For heaven's sake leave me alone!' he exclaimed, turning on her; 'have I not enough to bear already?'

'Yes,' she answered gravely, 'and the weight will be heavier if you are silent about its cause. If you will not tell the story, I shall, Carlo.'

She was not trembling then; her brother could see no emotion in the firm, proud mouth and white, determined face.

'Am I to go into Florence now?' he asked sullenly, glancing out on the approaching twilight.

'You can go when you like,' answered Lidia; 'but Marchese must know.'

'We shall meet him to-morrow night in the piazza,' said her brother.

She drew back.

'I cannot go up to Fiesole to-morrow,' she said, with a little catch in her voice.

'In that case I shall not see Vanutelli,'

replied Carlo, by no means delighted at the idea that Giulia Mirandoli might comment on their absence from the Fiesole villa, and draw her own conclusions therefrom. Then he altered his voice to a more subdued tone, guessing by instinct Lidia would not yield to tyranny. 'If you will go up to Fiesole,' he said, 'I will tell everything to Vanutelli in the evening; I should prefer to do so.'

He waited anxiously for her answer.

'Then I trust you to tell him everything,' she answered, 'and we will go to Fiesole to-morrow. We will not use the carriage, but go by train. As soon as you can you must arrange about selling the horses. You will thank Marchese for his noble generosity; you will ask his pardon for what you have done. Tell him no words can express your sorrow, and I—I too must ask him to forgive me for trusting my brother.'

She turned away very slowly. Carlo gave no answer, and Lidia went up to her studio. Only a few burning tears fell on her hands as she closed the windows to shut out the hot air. She brushed them away hastily. It was too late to paint, so she took up her sewing, and sat down to work.

* * * * *

Padre Antonio came to see Lidia the next morning while she was painting. He had been spending the night at Quaracchi, and wished to see her before he returned to Fiesole that day. He was greatly shocked at the pallor of her face, and though Lidia tried to be merry, and told him of her cousin's arrival and intention to stay in Florence, the old friar was not reassured. And then she asked him to pray for them very much; would he do so?

'Of course,' answered Padre Antonio, understanding that it had something to do with her white face.

'And there is someone else who needs your prayers, Padre,' she said. 'You know Signor Trerni, the English gentleman in our villa; he—he is an atheist.'

Padre Antonio's face became grave.

'I want you to pray for him,' she went on, looking up from her painting; 'he has been very kind to us.'

'He shall have the poor prayers I can

offer up,' replied the old friar, 'and also those of my community. Has he spoken to you of this?'

'Yes, once or twice,' she answered; 'it does not seem to tire him as it does Carlo. Last time he was here I do not think he was quite so incredulous.'

And she remembered Treherne had asked her if she ever prayed for those who did not believe.

'He does not try to convince you, child?' asked Padre Antonio anxiously.

Lidia shook her head, half smiling at the idea.

'How old is he?' asked the old priest abruptly.

'I do not know,' she answered. 'I never thought of it, but Albina calls him young.'

'Child,' said Padre Antonio after a pause, 'you must take care. There are many whose faith has been shaken while conversing with those more skilled in arguments than themselves. If you would convert the signore, you must pray for God's help to do so. Without it we are powerless, and if we do not ask God's blessing on our work, it is apt to be very imperfect.'

'"How old is he?" asked the old Priest abruptly.'—*Page* 162.

Lidia had bent her head over her palette. She now lifted it slowly.

'It is as you say, Padre,' she replied; 'but the Madonna will take care.'

'You are a good child,' said the old priest kindly, 'and you are right. We will pray to the Madonna for the Signor Inglese. The Feast of the Assumption is not far off. Her shrine is below your window. On that day I will offer up my Mass for the signore and your brother, and you will go to Communion; is it not so?'

'I will,' she replied eagerly.

'And,' went on Padre Antonio, half hesitating, 'if you could get the signore to go into a church on the Madonna's feast—— Very often she has taken pity on those blinded by their pride, when they enter into God's house.'

And then Padre Antonio took his leave.

As the hours wore by, Lidia grew more and more nervous at the idea of going up to the villa. Carlo, however, was so elated that he forgot his past humiliation and his sister's insane idea, as he called it, to take the tram into Florence.

As Lidia left the house with her brother,

Albina stood in front of the old Quaracchi farm, admiring her mistress as she walked down the road. She was looking very pretty. . Carlo was glad of this, for he was proud of his sister's appearance—it did him credit.

Miss Treherne was delighted to see them. Conte and Contessa Mirandoli were already there. They had found a dear little home, the Contessa declared gleefully. When they were settled, they must all come and see it. And how were Lidia and Carlo? Lidia was looking very tired—did not Miss Treherne think so? Treherne himself joined them at that moment, and then went off to fetch some wine for her, and throughout the visit took care of her in a way that made the little Contessa beam on him, and opened Carlo's eyes to another possibility.

They sat out on the terrace, shaded by a large awning. Lidia was content to listen to the others laughing and talking, while she herself looked over the city below and at San Miniato, where her mother lay buried.

To her relief, the visit she had paid to the villa was not alluded to. It was a happy day, Lidia felt, in spite of the many clouds that surrounded her. She grew lost in thought gazing at the view, knowing she would soon have to return home. This spoilt her, she knew, for the monotonous vineyards and distant hills at Quaracchi.

She was roused suddenly by Miss Treherne declaring it was time for them to start for Florence. Conte Mirandoli and Carlo announced their intention of walking down the hill, and the rest need not trouble about them.

As the carriage rolled down the broad zigzag road to the tune of the *cicade's* chatter, Lidia's sigh was very nearly approaching content. The air was full of balmy sweetness. The view from the hill was renowned for its incomparable beauty. San Miniato, with its stately cypresses, and farther on the smaller height of San Vito, were hardly distinguishable in the twilight. The towers and domes of Florence were lost in the deepening gloom over the hills beyond.

Lidia turned to make some remark on the beauty of the scene to Contessa Mirandoli, when she caught sight of Treherne's face opposite to her, and the words died away.

She had never seen such an expression on any face before. It frightened her, because at first she did not understand the uncertainty and longing, as though the mind were trying to see through some thick veil.

Treherne did not know that all the doubt and perplexity he had felt for many days now showed themselves in his face. It was the longing Lidia had spoken of, to thank someone for the beautiful scene before him; and she never forgot the expression she saw as they drove down into Florence.

Then, as they suddenly turned out of the Via Calzaioli into the magnificent Piazzi della Signoria, what a wonderful sight burst upon them! The Palazzo Vecchio, a stern gray pile, was one mass of flickering light. It was covered with countless little oil-lamps, which made the severe outlines of the building stand out in strong relief against the gloomy sky. The grand tower rose out of the clamouring crowd below up into the heavens, with tiny lights clinging to the sides. A feeling of awe and peace filled the hearts of those who gazed at the massive palazzo, that had stood for centuries, and witnessed the rise, zenith, and

'THE PALAZZO VECCHIO, A STERN GRAY PILE.'—*Page* 166.

fall of the city to which it belonged. It was on the piazza that many a fierce struggle had taken place between the two powerful factions of the Guelphs and the Ghibellines ; and it was from the prison-like windows of the palazzo that one of the Dukes of Medici threw his little son into the arms of an attendant below, so that the child should be as hardened to danger as his father.

At the Contessa's request, they all alighted and walked about among the gay throng of Florentines and peasants who had come from far to look on this sight. The chairs were thickly congregated outside the small *cafés*, brilliantly lighted up, and there Florentines discussed the beauty of the scene or the day's great heat, that had abated into a cool evening.

The Contessa was talking to Miss Treherne. Lidia was paying no attention to the conversation ; she was wondering with beating heart if Carlo had met Marchese Vanutelli and told him everything.

'Contessa, why did you do this ?' asked Treherne suddenly, just behind her.

She started round, not requiring to be told what he meant.

'Oh, signore,' she exclaimed, 'do not let us speak of it or refer to it again.'

'It shall be as you wish,' he answered gravely; 'we will act by your decision, and never refer to any of it again.'

'Oh no!' replied Lidia hastily; 'I did not mean that. I—you know——'

'Quite well,' answered the young man, smiling. 'How is my picture getting on?'

'It will not be finished for some time,' she answered. 'I hope you will be pleased with it, signore.'

There was a pause.

'Signore, I want you to do what I ask you,' she said timidly. 'You will not think it bold of me?'

She looked up at him to find he was watching her; she went on a little hurriedly when she saw the light shining in his eyes.

'You know, signore, the fifteenth of August is a great feast with us. We honour the Assumption on that day. The picture is in the "Madonna's Shrine" I painted. Will you —will you go into a church on that day and kneel for only a short time before the Santissimo? You need say no prayer, only look at the altar where God is. This is very bold of me, I fear; but oh, signore! you have been very kind to us. I want you to know God, and there is a story I heard once of a poor man who used to sit for many hours in a church, and when they asked him what he did without book or rosary, he said, " I look at Him, and He looks at me." The great faith of that poor man will help you.'

'If anything will help me,' said Treherne, 'it will be the great faith of a little girl called Contessa; and for all this what will be my reward?'

'Almighty God,' she answered simply.

'No, no,' he said; 'something else.'

'There is nothing more needed,' replied Lidia gravely. 'God fills the being, and satisfies every desire.'

They stood under the shade of the Loggia dei Lanzi. Treherne took her hand in his.

'Will you not give me this?' he asked in a low voice—'more precious to me than anything else in the world!'

Lidia started back, flushing crimson.

'Signore!' she exclaimed.

'What have I done?' asked Treherne, holding her hand tightly, 'beyond loving you with all my heart, and soul too, if I have one ?'

There was a deep silence which lasted many moments. Lidia's face had turned from crimson to white as snow; at last she found her voice.

'I am very sorry you should speak so, signore. If I had thought this would happen, I—I would not have come.'

'Then you would have been cruel!' he cried. 'What is there between us? When you are my wife, you can teach me your religion. Let me worship you now.'

'Oh, signore, do not say such wicked things!' she exclaimed, almost piteously, as she snatched her hand away from his. 'What are you doing? Mio Dio! You put me— His creature—in His holy place; me, who have no good in myself but what He has given me.'

'What does it matter what I said?' he answered. 'My darling, there is nothing between you and me.'

There was an agony of mingled doubt and certainty in his voice. Treherne began to be afraid Lidia would not listen to him. He was certainly very changed. In that eager face, with reverent love so plainly expressed in the eyes, there was little of the suspicious, cynical look it used to wear.

'There is God,' she replied very gravely, her brown eyes shining through her tears, and her lips quivering; 'God, who forbids such marriages.'

'Then but for Him you would hear me?' he exclaimed. 'If I believed as you do, Lidia, there would be nothing between us?'

The sweet face was very white as it turned towards the flickering lamps near them.

'You say right,' she answered, forgetting her English in her emotion, and speaking in a low voice. 'I do not know how to say it in your tongue, but—but you have been very kind. I—ti voglio molto bene' (I love you very much).

'I understand,' said Treherne, taking her hand and drawing it within his arm; 'there is nothing between us now.'

There was proud triumph in his eyes and voice.

'Oh, there is very much between us!' she

answered, a crimson flush spreading over her face; 'we must both be of the same faith, adoring the same God. No blessing comes of a marriage where God dwells not in the heart of both.'

And Lidia's face seemed transformed by a holy light. Treherne watched her with reverence and awe.

'You are saint enough for both of us,' he said.

'Oh, signore, do not say so!' she exclaimed earnestly. 'Were I a second St. Clare I should not be good enough. God wants us all for Himself, so great and infinite is His love.'

'Then you refuse me?' he asked, very slowly, as though to utter the words was great and bitter pain.

A gust of wind swept like a wave over the flickering illumination. For a few moments the lights wavered; Treherne could not see his companion's face in the darkness, and in those moments the agitation had passed away and all was calm again. They were standing alone by the beautiful Loggia dei Lanzi, under whose roof the famous statues looked weird and ghostly.

'Oh, come to us!' she cried suddenly. 'See, He is waiting for you—crying out to you to come to Him! Even now the Madonna is praying for you to her Son. Can you not believe? Oh, it seems all so plain!'

'Would that I had your wonderful faith!' exclaimed Treherne, in a stifled voice; 'it would destroy every barrier.'

'You must not wish it for that reason,' she answered; 'you must wish it for God's sake. Oh, signore, there is really no unbelief. Deep down in your heart God dwells, but so quietly, so silently, you do not know He is there. Pray; you will find Him very soon, and come to the church on the Madonna's feast.'

'I will,' he answered fervently, 'anything you wish.'

There was a short silence between them. Treherne drew her close to him.

'Oh, ti voglio molto bene!' she said, in a low voice so that he could hardly hear. 'Ma Dio! Dio soprattutto! (God above all things). Do you go to Ognissanti in the afternoon? You know where it is. I will be there.'

'Just as you wish,' he answered, thinking

to soothe and satisfy her by consenting, but having little thought of being converted. He loved and reverenced Lidia, but he thought her faith all imagination. 'But,' he went on, 'why not let it remain as it always has been? How can I change now? God, if there is a God, has waited for me long enough to come back.'

She shook her head.

'I cannot leave you so,' she answered, in an almost protecting tone. 'God waits for us to the very end—until we die; only when we stand before Him to be judged it will then be too late.'

'Where is Carlo? Have you seen Carlo and Bastiano?' asked the Contessa, suddenly appearing before them with Miss Treherne. She had left the two long enough, she decided. As it was, she had behaved as no Italian chaperon would behave; but Giulia Mirandoli was lenient when remembering her own early youth. 'It is quite time to be off. They joined us once, and now they have gone off again. You won't be home till to-morrow, Lidia. Where are the carriages?'

'I—we have not got ours,' stammered Lidia hastily.

'Madonna mia!' exclaimed the Contessa; 'and what are you going to do?'

'There is the tram,' began Lidia, when her eyes caught sight of the advancing group—there was Carlo, Bastiano, and Marchese. Miss Treherne and the Contessa turned to greet the latter cordially. Lidia stood alone, Treherne having left to see after his sister's carriage. Marchese Vanutelli made his way up to her, and held out his hand, smiling. Lidia put hers half mechanically into it, watching for any change in his face, but there was none. The rest were talking merrily. The Marchese drew her hand within his arm.

'Carlo tells me you did not bring the carriage with you,' he said. 'That was very foolish of you, Lidia; you must take mine.' And he led her towards it.

When she was able to speak, Lidia gasped out:

'I cannot—oh, Marchese! I——'

'You will do what I tell you,' he answered quietly as he put her in. 'You can shelter it for the night, can you not? Have you enjoyed yourself, bimba?'

Tears filled the large brown eyes.

'Yes,' she answered, 'thank you—thank you very much! I want you to come to Quaracchi to-morrow, will you?'

He bowed his head, and then turned away from the carriage as the rest came up to bid her good-bye.

The lonely Quaracchi road was lighted by dancing fireflies as the brother and sister drove home in silence.

They flew about, appearing and disappearing in the wake of the carriage. The stars were shining overhead, and these little stars in the country roads were lighting up the dark ditches and solitary ways.

CHAPTER X.

MARCHESE VANUTELLI was on the veranda waiting to see the Contessina, Albina told her young mistress the next morning, and added she did not know what he would say when he saw her looking so ill. And, indeed, the Marchese was startled as Lidia came forward to greet him; for her smile did not hide the dark lines under her eyes or the pallor of her face.

'You are not well, Lidia!' he exclaimed, taking her hand, and seeing these changes with anxiety and pain.

'Oh, it is nothing,' she answered hastily, though she could not conceal her agitation. 'Marchese, Carlo has told you everything,' she went on, flushing crimson with shame. 'It is kind of you—it is very like you to treat us still as friends.'

'What is the matter?' he asked gravely. 'You are not yourself, child.'

'Did he tell you?' she asked, taking no notice of his words; then, with piteous distress, 'Marchese, you do not mean to say Carlo never told you?'

'Bimba!' he exclaimed anxiously, and wishing he did know, so as to save her the trouble of telling him. 'What is it? I do not understand.'

Lidia's hands fell powerless to her side.

'Lidia,' said the Marchese sharply, on seeing the white quivering face, 'what has the boy been doing to grieve you now? Tell me, carina! tell me!'

'He had no work,' she answered in a low voice, determined to go through the confession bravely. 'He has—he has deceived you, Marchese. You kept the horses for me. I did not know it. God will reward you for all your goodness. We cannot. We have repaid it with deception. Marchese, forgive us——'

'Do not say any more, child,' he interrupted.

There was a pause. Marchese Vanutelli

was too much engrossed in his anxiety for her to think of the wrong done to himself. It was the same as it always was—as it always would be. While he walked up and down the veranda beside her, he forgot himself in trying to make things brighter for her. Though no tears came, her silent grief distressed him, as did her humble prayer for forgiveness, as though she had been a partner in the deceit.

'It was no good trying!' she exclaimed. 'O Dio mio! how could he have done it? And to you, Marchese, who have been so good to us!'

'I am thankful he should have come to me and no one else,' he answered. 'Do not take this so much to heart, Lidia. Now that we know the truth, we will take more care of the boy in future, that no strong temptations may come in his way. Child, look up and say you will try not to grieve. Far above his deceiving me, I am angry at the way he has made you suffer.'

'It has always been the same,' she said in a trembling voice. 'You always forget yourself for others, Marchese.'

There was a pause. Then he took her hands in his own.

'Piccina, you will let me take care of you till I die?' he said.

'Take care of me,' she repeated, misunderstanding him. 'You have done so, Marchese.'

'You will give me the right, Lidia?' he said, bending down to her. 'Do you not understand? I want you to be my wife!'

She looked up at him quickly, and clasped her hands in bewildered distress. Marchese loved her! He wanted her to be his wife. It came upon her suddenly—this wonderful change in their old friend. Many times she opened her lips to speak, but the words would not come.

'I have distressed you!' he exclaimed. 'Forgive me, carina! I thought you must have guessed.'

'Oh, Marchese!' she cried, tears filling her eyes, 'why have you done this? Why have you done this?'

'Why!' repeated the Marchese, a strange tightening in his heart. 'Oh, child! how can you ask me? If I have spoken of a thing repugnant to you, do not fear to say so.'

And he stood watching her—very quietly, an on-looker might have said, for all the tumult within was hidden from sight. Without speaking, she looked up at him, and then held out her hand.

The Marchese took it quietly in his own. Many might have misunderstood the gesture, but not Marchese Vanutelli. He knew why and how the hand was offered, and he guessed instinctively what had passed in the Piazza della Signoria only the night before. Perhaps some would have said his face did not change, for he was in the shadow, and the terrible grayness was hidden, so was the look of age—and, oh, such age!—that spread over his features.

'I have understood my answer,' he spoke at last, striving to regain his ordinary voice, so as not to distress or frighten her, and wishing to save her the pain of speaking. 'Do not grieve any more. I will not speak of this or trouble you again. Once more I am your friend, bimba, in whom you must confide.'

'Marchese,' she faltered, 'forgive me if—if I ever led you to believe my answer would be different to what it is.'

'Do not think that, or I shall never forgive myself,' he answered. 'You had every right to come to me; had you not done so, I should have been very grieved. Your mother confided you to my care. Do not let this come between us, child. Forget all I have said, and tell me what distresses you just as you would if I had not spoken.'

The Marchese's voice trembled a little at the last words, and he stood waiting for the old confidence to come back again. It is true great pain was tearing at his heart, but he forced it down; there was her happiness to think of before his own.

For many moments Lidia could not speak, and then something told her the Marchese would be more grieved at her silence than if she spoke, and Lidia's trembling voice broke the stillness at last. And as she told the story, little by little, the old childish trust in Marchese came back, and nothing was kept from him: Treherne's wish for her to be his wife —her own wish—but where her duty lay. They could never be married while he denied God.

The Marchese was silent for a few moments.

The look of age had deepened, but his voice was as brave and firm as ever.

'Bimba, you will trust me to help you. You must not grieve any more. I will try and help you as far as I can.'

'I have grieved you, Marchese. I should have been silent about it!' she exclaimed, catching sight of his face. 'But God and the Madonna must love you very much—and who am I?'

For one short moment it seemed as if the passionate Italian nature must break forth from the will that held it so firmly in curb, but the Marchese's noble unselfishness conquered.

'You are to be my little friend, bimba; is it not so?' he answered. 'Do not let me go away with the knowledge I have distressed you. The day will come when you will be very happy among those you love. You must spare yourself the trouble of speaking to Carlo. Where is he?'

'I think—I think he has gone out,' she faltered.

'Then perhaps I shall meet him on my way home,' he said. 'Addio for a little while.'

'For a little while,' she repeated, holding out her hand.

Something in the tone of her voice made him say:

'I am not leaving Florence, child, yet. I must stay on and see if all is well with you. So we will say "a rivederci."'

'Thank you, Marchese,' she answered. 'God bless you very much!'

He was still his quiet self when he took her hand and bade her good-bye. He left the old Quaracchi farm very silently too, but Albina, who saw him go, said that Marchese Vanutelli's figure was bowed, and that his face, as he passed out of the house, was like that of a dead man—white and motionless.

* * * * *

The sun was shining full on the Villa Donati as Marchese Vanutelli walked up the old cypress avenue. He paused before ringing the bell, and glanced round half mechanically; but he was himself in a moment. What had been his promise to her mother? Before the thought for her happiness all others should give way. And his happiness—what was his happiness compared to hers?

In a few moments he had entered the house, and very soon afterwards Treherne came to him. The young man drew back in utter astonishment. It is true the Marchese came forward very quietly to greet him, but his face was drawn and gray; there was a certain hesitation in his manner as he extended his hand to Treherne, though it disappeared when he grasped his friend's warmly.

'I must surprise you by this visit, signore,' said the Marchese. 'You will forgive me if what I am going to say seems as if I were prying too much into your affairs, but I feel that I must speak, and ask you to do your duty towards God and yourself.'

Treherne was too surprised to give any answer, and the Marchese continued:

'Before she died, the Marchesa Donati confided her daughter to my care. She asked me to act for her happiness, and I gave my promise to her. Lidia has told me of your wish, and—and her wish, and of what is between you. Signore, her earthly happiness lies in your hands. She will never draw back from her resolution rather to sacrifice her hopes than offend God by uniting herself to one who despises Him. My desire is for her welfare, but I know well she would enjoy very little true happiness were you shut out from God. You would have no sympathies with her, for her religion is part of herself—her one great aim. Confidence must exist between husband and wife in all things, and God must reign over both. It is He who joins you together, and blesses a good marriage with happiness. Do not misunderstand me; I would not wish you to profess, for the sake of gaining her consent, a religion in which you do not believe—that would be a sacrilegious hypocrisy; but I beg of you to ask yourself seriously whether it is really from conviction that you do not believe in your Creator, or whether pride has not prompted your denial, as it has prompted so many others, who have at last humbled themselves on their death-beds, when their Creator was about to become their Judge.'

The Marchese paused, and looked earnestly at the young man, as though expecting an answer, but Treherne did not reply. He felt by instinct that Vanutelli loved Lidia, and that it was unselfish love which had brought him up to the villa, and this knowledge brought him face to face with a truth which he had not before realized. If he, the unbeliever, could not win Lidia, she might in time reward the one who was indeed worthier of her than he was; and yet that one was here even now, sacrificing himself in order to work for her interests, and using his utmost endeavours to bring about a union which would destroy his own hopes. Surely Marchese Vanutelli could not so forget himself without the help of some power above nature. Was it his religion which inspired such noble and unselfish conduct? Was he (Treherne) to own himself in the wrong, after all?

The Marchese spoke again—this time in a strange, hard voice, as though he had put himself under a rigid control:

'You are young; life's happy prime is still before you. With Lidia Donati for your wife you will indeed enjoy a heaven on earth. Once you have known her, can you doubt the existence of God? Can you say you are happier than those who, like her, are filled with God's peace, which the world cannot give or take away? Are you wiser than all those men of intellect and learning who have gone before you, serving and adoring Him who created them? Do not waste and ruin your life. You cannot ruin hers, for she has placed it in God's keeping, but you can fill it with bitter sorrow. She will grieve at not becoming your wife, though, to a woman such as she is, that will be secondary to the terrible thought that the one she loves is shut out from God's sight.'

Treherne advanced slowly towards the Marchese with outstretched hand. In how many cases a noble deed has done more good than eloquent words! And the brave example before him made the first wish to know this great God dawn in Treherne's heart. He had wished it the night before, only that Lidia might be his wife, but as he held out his hand he longed to adore the One whom he had hitherto denied, and his cold doctrine was for the first time repugnant to him.

'Thank you for your kindness, Marchese,' he said, much moved. 'I will try. And if—if I come to believe in time as you do, it will have been you and Lidia who have worked the change.'

The Marchese's eyes were dim with emotion, and he could hardly see the figure standing before him; but with his iron will he crushed out the last attempt of his nature to conquer his bravery.

'Dio le benedica!' he said in his native tongue, as he held the hand of one who from that hour ranked as his friend, and ever after loved him as such.

Once in his own room in the great palazzo, Marchese Vanutelli paced up and down, wrestling with himself. But even a brave nature has its limits of endurance. The Marchese stopped suddenly in his walk. A remembrance of his plans of decorating and enlivening the old palazzo for his wife came back to him. For a moment he was motionless. There was a portrait on the wall just above, gazing down on him with sad and wistful eyes. It was the Marchese's mother. Looking up, he met their gaze. The silent sympathy, though it was only from a portrait, unnerved him. He sank down into a chair underneath his mother's picture, and buried his face in his arms, resting on the table. Shall we let the curtain fall? There are some great and passionate griefs on which God only has the right to look.

* * * * *

Carlo had gone away. The truth forced itself on Lidia as she waited anxiously until dusk crept on for her brother's return. When he left her that morning, saying he might be home at any time, it was his intention to go away and not come back again. Lidia did not know what to do, she was so terrified and anxious. All that night she kept watch in the studio, Albina endeavouring to calm her mistress's excitement.

'He will return to-morrow,' she kept on saying. 'Perhaps he has met a friend in Florence who has persuaded him to remain the night in his house.'

But Lidia would not be reassured. Morning came, and there was still no Carlo; and, forgetting all that had passed between herself and their old friend, she sent a message begging him to come to her. He was Marchese, the one to whom she always turned for help before anyone else, and it was Marchese who came out to Quaracchi immediately he received the summons. He was glad to see when she came to meet him that the old childish confidence was still there.

'Tell me everything, bimba,' he said.

She obeyed, and told the story almost incoherently, so great was her anxiety; but the Marchese understood. He promised to look for Carlo immediately. He would send Contessa Mirandoli to her from Florence. And it was Marchese who bought the horses and carriage from her, seeing how much she wished to be rid of them.

Throughout the interview he was quite the same; only now and then, when Lidia was overpowered with distress, did he show any signs of how much he suffered; but the emotion was checked almost as soon as it came. Already Marchese Vanutelli looked on her as the wife of another.

'You must trust me to see about it all,' he said gravely. 'Is it not so, child? We will say "a rivederci" now. Do not be too anxious; the boy has not gone very far. When I find him, I will bring him back, and look after him in future, and see that he is strong in all his trials.'

Lidia followed him down to the little vineyard door, as usual, and bade him good-bye there. She could not thank him for all he had done, and the Marchese understood that her gratitude was speechless. There may be some who would have said his farewell was even cold, but he had put himself under a rigid control, knowing very well, if he once gave way to his hot Italian nature he could never recover himself, but would bring sorrow on the one he loved.

'A rivederci,' he said quietly, holding out his hand. 'God bless you, child!'

Lidia saw him, but dimly through the misty tears, get into his carriage, that had driven him so quickly to the Quaracchi farm. She watched him disappear, then turned to go down the road towards the Madonna's shrine. She knelt down on the stone in the lonely country lane, and looked through the iron grating at the picture within. Something caught her eyes at the foot of the painting. She looked closer. It was the little pearl earring she had given Marchese lying half hidden by the masses of flowers.

CHAPTER XI.

It was a burning August day. A hot sirocco was blowing on the broad Lung' Arno and in the narrow streets. The grand ceremony that had been taking place in the church of Ognissanti was just over. Those who had crowded in were going out between the rows of beggars at the doors.

The sacristan, in his white dress, was inside putting out the many brilliant lights that every moment threatened to set fire to the red and gold draperies with which the Italians always decorate their churches on great feasts; and it *was* a great feast—the fifteenth of August.

A few peasants lingered on still before the altars. There were a good many in the right transept kneeling before the Blessed Sacrament. The red lamp burned dim in the dark that shut in the altar. At the sanctuary barrier within them knelt a solitary figure in black.

The worshippers came and moved away silently, leaving Lidia still kneeling motionless. A great many wondered who that black figure could be, kneeling there alone.

A beggar, holding her baby in her arms, went up to her with outstretched hand, murmuring some words intended to excite the pious signora's pity; but Lidia did not hear her, and the beggar woman went away.

After a little while Lidia lifted her head; several others looked up, too, as the tall figure of a gentleman came towards them — an unusual sight in an Italian church at that hour. He immediately saw Lidia, and went up to her. She held out her hand to him in greeting, and those who watched saw her smile. There were many peasants there who left the church saying they had seen a saint. One imaginative old woman said that they were husband and wife—that the thoughtful husband had come to fetch his wife home. But the lady did not go away, and the husband knelt down on one knee beside her.

The wonderful silence around, the solitary lamp burning steadily in the gloom, awed the heart of the unbeliever. He remembered the story of the poor man: 'I sit and look at Him, and He looks at me.' Was there really a God? Was it to be that one day, sooner or later, he would turn to this unknown God, whose power none could resist, as Marchese Vanutelli had said? Did that great God really dwell in the tabernacle and hear the prayers of the silent worshippers?

Treherne looked back over centuries of time. The Church to which Lidia belonged had always remained the same, holding the same doctrine, adoring God hidden in the Blessed Sacrament. All other religions had fallen away, had divided into sects, until the original doctrine had been quite lost; but this Church, that they said God Himself had raised, remained the same through many and great dangers. And in his happiest moments was he as happy as those who the Marchese said possessed a peace that the world cannot give or take away?

He looked down at the kneeling figure by his side. She, whom he loved more than he could ever say, was bending down before this great, unseen, and wonderful God, whose existence he denied, and for whom Lidia would unhesitatingly give him up unless he believed as she did. And he was kneeling too—he wondered why. It had seemed natural to him on entering the chapel to do so—and why? Treherne could not tell. The faith of Lidia Donati was not of man—no one was ever so wrapped up in anything that did not exist as she was in her religion. It needed some wonderful power to put it there. Surely Lidia would not kneel and adore before an empty shrine! The idea that her faith was born of imagination began to melt away. There was Marchese Vanutelli's example, too, ever before his eyes. What had prompted his unselfish sacrifice and helped him to carry it out?

There was a barrier between himself and Lidia that he only could remove. The Marchese had asked him not to ruin his own life. He had said that Lidia's was safe, for she had placed it in God's keeping.

The daylight was beginning to fade, but still Lidia remained motionless—dead to all outward things—rapt in prayer for the two beings she loved best in all the world.

He put his hand on her arm. She looked up.

'I will come,' she said, and rose with difficulty, being cramped from kneeling on the cold stone.

She knelt down again, and he stood waiting for her. It seemed as though she could not tear herself away. The few who still remained watched the two walk slowly from the chapel.

'How will you get home?' he asked anxiously, as they stood in the porch.

She pointed to a cab standing near the church. He signed it to approach and put her into it.

'Your brother——' He hesitated, looking with pain on her white face, which contracted at the words.

'No; he has not returned,' she answered, in a low voice. 'Giulia, my cousin, is still with me. Thank you for coming, signore; God will reward you.'

'And you?' he asked quickly.

'God will reward you,' she repeated, looking up at him with her grave eyes; 'I have nothing——'

'And when you give yourself to me,' he said, 'do you think that will be nothing?'

'Oh no!' she answered, her voice quivering, 'for—ti voglio tanto bene. It is no reward.'

The Contessa herself helped Lidia from the carriage at the Quaracchi farm.

'No, piccina, he has not come back.' She answered the unspoken question that was written so plainly on her cousin's face. 'The Marchese was here while you were away. I wish you had let me go with you, Lidia, instead of waiting at home for the boy. You are looking so white and tired.'

* * * * *

Lidia was putting the finishing strokes to her picture two days after the feast. She was very pale from great suffering, though she said nothing about it, thinking it was only ordinary rheumatism from kneeling on the cold stone in the church for so long. She wanted to finish her picture that day; the Contessa had gone to Florence in the afternoon, and so was not there to forbid her to work.

The brush dropped at last from her helpless hands, and she sat shivering before the easel, turning first hot, then cold. She bent her head down in her hands.

'O God!' she moaned, 'accept this pain for their conversion.'

· She rose painfully from her stool, the room turning round and round before her. She could not see her picture, though she stood quite near it; a thick mist seemed to have come before her eyes.

Very slowly Lidia walked to the door and went downstairs to ask Albina for a little wine; but she forgot all about it on arriving in the hall below, and thought she would go to the drawing-room and await the Contessa's return from Florence. Some of Carlo's bills were lying on the table in the middle of the room. She sank down into a chair, holding them in her trembling hand, and began to add them up to see if they really amounted to the large sum at the bottom of the column of figures.

Suddenly she started to her feet. Footsteps and voices in the hall attracted her attention. She heard the Contessa speaking in a low, angry voice; then someone answered in the same tone. Lidia ran over to the door, her heart beating violently. She caught at the handle for support; the rushing sound in her ears increased—a double veil blinded her eyes. There was total darkness round her as she fell heavily to the ground.

CHAPTER XII.

THE next morning after Carlo's sudden reappearance Lidia lay on her bed, tortured by the agonizing pains of rheumatic fever. The Contessa, frightened beyond all measure, conquered her determination never to speak to Carlo again, and ordered him to go into Florence for the doctor. Carlo obeyed. His absence from home had not sweetened his disposition, and he only returned to Quaracchi because he had no more money. On entering the house he had faced his cousin in the hall, and her sharp taunts did not tend to soften his nature. He knew he had gone away because he was afraid to meet his sister's just anger, and because he knew Marchese Vanutelli would take good care no further deceit should be practised; there was no need for the Contessa to remind him

After having seen Carlo, Giulia Mirandoli went back to Lidia's room and found her cousin eager to hear all about Carlo, in spite of her pain. The Contessa said there was nothing to tell her—he was not worth speaking of; and Albina, who was also in the room, agreed by nodding her head vigorously. Lidia looked at them in silence, and stifled a sigh.

'Piccina, do not grieve so!' exclaimed the Contessa quickly. 'You——'

'Ah! what is that?' cried Lidia. She tried to start up to listen, but sank back with a bitter cry of pain.

'Cara signorina, do not move,' said Albina; 'I think it is the Signor Inglese.'

At a sign from the Contessa, Albina left the room and met Treherne coming up the stairs.

'You cannot see the Contessa,' she exclaimed quickly; 'she is too ill. It would excite her.'

She pointed to the door of Lidia's room, then shook her head at Treherne, who turned very white, and repeated:

'She is too ill! What is it?'

'IN THE FOREGROUND WAS THE FACE THAT FASCINATED TREHERNE.'
Page 203.

'Signore can go into the studio,' said Albina, 'and the Contessa Giulia will explain everything if he will wait in there a little while.'

She opened the door of Lidia's studio for Treherne to enter, then ran back to her mistress to find her eyes bright and wide open, and a flush of excitement on her cheek. She heard his step in the next room, but said nothing. The wise Albina was silent, too, as Contessa Mirandoli slipped away.

The picture Lidia had painted stood on the easel in the window. Treherne went listlessly towards it. He paused thunderstruck when his eyes fell on the painting, which was indeed a wonderful one. It represented a wayside crucifix, weather-beaten, and damaged by many a storm. Before it knelt an old peasant, whose withered face was uplifted in reverence and love to the figure on the cross, and whose bony hands were clasped in humble supplication. A little behind him in the foreground was the face that fascinated Treherne. It was that of a young man in the dress of the sixteenth century, evidently of rich and noble birth, to judge by his handsome features and costly dress. He had apparently paused in his walk to look back on the old man praying, and over his face had crept the wonderful expression that made the picture a masterpiece. It was full of unsatisfied longing, as though the heart beneath had sought after peace and had not found it. That look eclipsed all else save the demon of mockery that lurked about his mouth at the sight of religion he had seen fit to scoff at all his life as others did, but which deep down in his heart he knew was good and true. Treherne understood the meaning of it immediately: 'The believer and the unbeliever.'

'Lidia has painted that young man very like you, signore,' said the Contessa's voice just behind him.

He started round, then looked at the picture again. He did not know that Lidia had copied the expression she had seen on his face.

'It is very beautiful,' he said, half mechanically; then rousing himself, 'Is she very ill, Contessa? You must write me out a list of what she would be likely to want, and I will see about it in Florence immediately.'

The Contessa was greatly touched. She did not need to be told this young Englishman had fallen in love with her cousin. After that there was nothing Lidia wanted or the doctor ordered her that she did not get. Miss Treherne used to drive over every day, always bringing some new luxury for the sufferer. Her brother often stayed all night in the studio, listening for any change, or to know if anything was wanted in Florence. In the daytime Conte Mirandoli was always ready to go on any errand. A nun, sent by Padre Antonio, came to nurse Lidia, and only she the Contessa, and Albina, were allowed inside the sick-room by the doctor. During her nights of delirium Treherne paced up and down the room, trying not to hear her cries for fear the temptation to go to her would overpower him, yet unable to tear himself away from the studio, where Lidia's picture was his companion.

There was another, too, who never failed in his daily visits and inquiry after the invalid, but only Albina knew of his coming and going at the little vineyard door. Always after those visits Albina's eyes were very misty, and, strange to say, the tears were not for the Contessina. It was the only time in the day the good-hearted woman forgot her young mistress, and had you asked her why she cried, she would most likely have said, 'Chi lo sa?' She would walk very slowly back to the old white farmhouse, and say to herself how fond the Marchese always was of the Contessina; but the real truth was hidden even from her, though she saw him every day.

One morning Treherne drove up to the door of the Quaracchi home. Before the Madonna's shrine knelt a peasant-girl sobbing bitterly.

'O Madonna, Madonna! salvatela!' (save her!).

He went quickly up to her. Her face was buried in her arms, resting on the stone shrine.

'What has happened?' he asked.

'Oh, the Contessina!' cried the girl, turning a tear-stained face and red eyes towards him. 'In the night she was very ill—she is dying! Padre Antonio is coming; they have sent for him to the monastery. He is going to give her the Santissimo.'

'BEFORE THE MADONNA'S SHRINE KNELT A PEASANT GIRL.'—*Page* 206.

'But she was better yesterday,' said Treherne, in a strange, hard voice.

'Yes, it was so,' replied the *contadina;* 'but in the night she grew worse; and oh, signore! I am praying to the Madonna, who gave me my Luigi.'

It was Beppa, the model in the 'Madonna's Shrine,' who knelt before him. He passed by her quickly, and entered the house, where all was silent.

Albina came to meet him with a white and frightened face.

'Oh, signore!' she exclaimed on seeing him, 'what can we do? The Contessina is worse, and the doctor went back to Florence last evening. The Conte has not been to Quaracchi to-day, and we cannot send the Signor Marchese away from his sister.'

Treherne had already half turned away.

'I will go,' he answered in a stifled voice, as he realized he should have to leave her in danger. 'Do not be afraid. I will bring the doctor back with me.'

'Oh, may God reward you, signore!' cried the distressed servant. 'You will go quickly, will you not?'

Treherne made a hurried answer and left the house.

Beppa was still sobbing before the shrine, heedless of the sun that was pouring down on her bare head.

Treherne only half glanced at her, then turned to enter his carriage, when a voice close by called his name. He turned round hastily and confronted Marchese Vanutelli, who had just come up the road. Grief-stricken as he was, Treherne could not fail to notice the change in the other's face; the Marchese looked as if twenty years had been added to his five-and-thirty.

'She is worse!' he exclaimed, coming towards the young man and speaking in a voice that sounded to the one who listened as if it were muffled. 'And you are going for the doctor? You must not do so. Stay with her—it is your duty.'

'I know,' burst out Treherne passionately; 'and I would not leave if I were not obliged. But the doctor is wanted—there is no one——'

'Yes,' interrupted the Marchese quietly; 'I am here. Let me go instead of you.'

He laid his hand on the young man's arm and drew him back from the carriage.

'If—if anything happened,' went on the Marchese in a voice that quivered ever so little, 'you would be the first to be called; I—I should be the last.'

Treherne hardly knew what happened then, except that he allowed himself to be led back to the house again, where the Contessa was standing in the hall. She came swiftly towards him.

'I am so glad you did not go!' she exclaimed. 'Albina told me she had sent you for the doctor. Lidia has been asking for you. Follow me. Do not talk too much to her.'

The Contessa's voice trembled very much. Unable to question her, Treherne did as she told him. Carlo was standing by his sister's bed when they entered.

Treherne just caught her faintly-uttered words:

'Oh, Carlo, promise me!'

Her brother drew back to let his friend take his place by Lidia's side. Treherne saw nothing in the dark room except the white, terribly white face on the pillow, and the dying light in the brown eyes.

'Come near,' she said faintly. 'How is it with you?'

'Oh, my precious one!' he exclaimed, bending over her. 'Tell me how *you* are!'

'I cannot say I am better,' she answered. 'Oh, Francesco, if God sees fit to take me, will you love Him? I have prayed—and Carlo—Carlo too.'

Marchese Donati could not withstand the imploring look in his sister's eyes. He broke down suddenly and fell on his knees; Treherne, who felt so calm now, wondered at his emotion; but after a few moments he cried out passionately, carried away by the immense grief of losing her:

'How can He exist if He does not save you?'

'Oh, do not say that!' she exclaimed, speaking slowly and with difficulty, her brown eyes shining up at him. 'It is God's will. Do not let me come between Almighty God and you. He is about to come to me soon to help me on the great journey I may have to go.

You will stay, Francesco, and believe. God is very good. He will not refuse me. I have loved you very much. Oh, Giulia! mia cara!' she exclaimed as the Contessa, seated in a chair behind Treherne, sobbed convulsively.

'Come over here, mia bimba,' said Lidia, trying to smile. 'Where is Bastiano?'

'He will come, carina; he will come,' answered the Contessa, battling down her grief.

'And—and Marchese?' asked Lidia. 'I should like to see Marchese.' She looked up at Treherne, who remembered with remorse what he had allowed Lidia's friend to do for him.

'He has gone for the doctor, my darling,' he answered in a stifled voice; 'he went instead of me.'

'Then—then you will tell him that I could never thank him enough,' she said; 'that —that his kindness to us—to me, above everyone, I am not able to repay. Oh, Francesco, you will love Marchese very much, will you not?'

Treherne's answer was inaudible.

'I hear them coming!' exclaimed Lidia, her face lighting up. 'God is coming!'

Treherne fell on his knees beside her, and, burying his face in his arms against the bed, burst into passionate sobs.

'Oh, call on the Madonna,' she murmured. 'She will hear.'

Then all was silence, till Padre Antonio entered with his attendants bearing the Sacred Host.

Treherne's eyes met a very solemn sight when he next looked up. A temporary altar had been made, on which lighted candles were burning. They were all there—Carlo, Conte Mirandoli and his wife, the nursing sister, Albina and Beppa, with some others he did not know. His eyes wandered to Lidia's face—it was indeed transformed with love and desire.

The Contessa was bowed to the very ground; Treherne could hear her praying to God to have mercy on Lidia and save her. Albina and Beppa were calling on the Madonna; even Marchese Donati's head was bowed, his lips were moving, and Conte Mirandoli was praying too. And to whom could Treherne go for help? The picture she had painted for him rose up before his eyes—the loving, trustful face of the poor *contadino*, the restless longing for peace in the countenance of the young noble.

Padre Antonio was repeating, 'Domine, non sum dignus.' A strange new feeling came over Treherne, and then he bent his head. He could not help it. The same impulse that prompted him to kneel in the chapel at Ognissanti overpowered him then. A nameless awe filled the heart of the unbeliever. In that moment when Lidia Donati was dying Francis Treherne knelt and adored the God Whose existence he had denied—to Whom he had never turned since he was a child.

The existence of God filled his being, as Lidia had said; he was dead to all else save the prayer for Lidia's life, which was the first he uttered: 'My God, save her!' And who knows that God in His infinite mercy was not waiting for that prayer to answer their petition?

What passed between God and the soul of him who now believed we cannot say. There are many things too sacred to be written down. We will not speak of what followed in that silent room.

Padre Antonio roused Treherne by touching him on the shoulder.

'Signore, will you not come?' he said; 'she is now sleeping peacefully. It is the first rest she has had for some time. It may be the will of God to save her.'

He spoke in Italian. Treherne only half understood, and rose to his feet.

There was only the nursing sister, seated at the foot of Lidia's bed, and themselves in the dark room. Her eyes were closed, she was breathing slowly and regularly. In her hand she held a little wooden Crucifix.

'Oh, my God, save her!' he exclaimed again.

'The Madonna will have pity,' murmured the nun, looking with compassion on the young man, whose devotion and reverence had surprised her. 'Do not fear; the Contessa is now sleeping peacefully.'

Once outside the door of the sick-room, Padre Antonio turned to his companion.

'Signore,' he began hesitatingly, 'this is

the first time I have been able to speak to you. Will you answer my question? You are going to make Lidia your wife. She told me you did not believe in God. Is that so?'

'It is over now,' answered Treherne gravely.

The old friar clasped his thin brown hands.

'I am very pleased,' he said, in quaintly spoken English, tears shining in his eyes. 'God bless you, my son! and make your life with your lady a long and happy one.'

* * * * *

Lidia Donati passed safely through the crisis of her illness. There was no need now to fear her being a cripple, though once the doctor gave up all hope and said she would never walk again. A week had passed since she was able to leave her bed. The doctor still forbade any kind of excitement; the room was only open to the nursing sister and Contessa Mirandoli, whose services were invaluable, and, indeed, you would never have thought the lively little lady could be so subdued and clever in a sick-room. Her husband listened, half smiling, to all the praises of her nursing, and was surprised they should not have found out sooner that trait in the Contessa's nature.

Carlo had grown very quiet and grave lately, seldom taking any notice of anyone. The *salone* was generally empty, and he spent his days there. He grew restless as Lidia got better, and seemed to be waiting for someone who never came. At last a bitter, remorseful feeling had awakened in Marchese Donati's heart. He could not rid himself of the idea which had assailed him the day his sister was dying, that much of the severity of her illness was owing to him, and that he had acted in a far from honourable manner. A spark of dormant honour had suddenly been rekindled within him. He seemed to realize how he had behaved towards the friend who was so ready to help him, and Carlo bowed his head on the table near which he was sitting one morning in the *salone*, and allowed shame to overpower him. He felt he could never face Marchese Vanutelli again, though he longed to see him and make some little atonement to the man who had been so generous towards him, and whom he had so wantonly deceived.

All his past faults rose up before him and

overwhelmed him. After all, it was he who had killed his mother by his cowardly selfishness, and brought his sister very nearly to her grave. A convulsive shudder ran through the young man. He was so overpowered with remorse that had been growing greater every day, and now had reached its highest pitch, that he did not hear footsteps behind him—only felt a hand laid on his shoulder; and when that had roused him, though he did not move, he heard a voice say:

'Look up, my boy; your punishment has been great enough, God knows.'

And, turning round, he confronted Marchese Vanutelli. He rose. The words refused to come when he saw his friend's altered face.

'Your punishment is very great,' repeated the Marchese gravely, yet glad to see this sudden change for the better. 'If you want me to forgive you, Carlo, I do so with all my heart. Your wrong to your sister has been greater than your wrong to me. Had you been more careful of her, and less so of yourself, her illness would probably not have been so severe. I do not wish to say hard things to you, my boy, but the truth must be brought home to us sometimes, if we do not realize it ourselves. Please God, now all will be well with her. She will be very happy with—with one who loves her so dearly as Signor Treherne. It is you we must think of now, Carlo, for you will be left alone. If you will come to me, it will give me great pleasure to help you in your life until you can make a home of your own.'

Touched as he was by the generous offer, Carlo could not reply; but it roused all his better nature, and brought it to the fore sooner than angry words and bitter reproaches would have done. For some time he could not find his voice, though the Marchese was waiting for his answer.

'I cannot,' he replied in a strained voice. 'I have already behaved most dishonourably towards you. I——'

'Put that aside,' interrupted the Marchese; 'there is no need to refer to it again. We are to be friends, Carlo, and forget all that has passed.'

'No,' replied Carlo firmly; 'I must not forget all I have done. I must make amends.

You know, Marchese, I cannot thank you enough. But I think it would be better to remain on in Quaracchi, and go into Florence to work; that is, if—if you can trust me to do so.'

Marchese Vanutelli held out his hand.

'I can,' he answered quietly; 'and you are doing your duty in deciding upon this plan. I am leaving Florence for a little while; when I come back I shall find you—you all very happy.'

Carlo did not notice the tremor in his friend's voice, for it was very slight; but he saw the look of age and grayness that came over the Marchese's face. He was going to ask if his friend was unwell, but something seemed to check the question, and, after all, the change soon passed.

'You will bid good-bye to Lidia for me,' went on the Marchese in his ordinary voice; 'it is better she should not be disturbed. She is getting better now, and has kind friends in whose charge I can leave her without fear. Addio, Carlo.'

Half mechanically, Carlo put out his hand. He seemed to guess something was sending

Marchese Vanutelli away from Florence for a long time, but he shrank from asking the cause. Altogether it was a very different Carlo who held out his hand to the one who had run away from home some time before.

'You will bid good-bye to all my friends for me,' went on the Marchese. 'I am leaving Florence for Sicily; if you ever want me, you will write to me at Casa Grande, Palermo —it will find me.'

'Are you—are you going for a long time?' asked Carlo, wondering what this great change meant.

The Marchese did not immediately reply; his eyes wandered out into the vineyard, to the little green door where he was standing when Lidia became his all to him, and where he had inquired every day after her. For a long time was it to be? Yes, it would be better so, till he got over it. He left her in good hands, among those who would love her as her mother would wish.

'I suppose Signor Treherne is not at Quaracchi yet?' he asked, seeming to have forgotten the question put to him. 'I should like to have seen him before I left Florence.'

No; Carlo did not think Treherne had come yet.

'I may meet him on the way,' said the Marchese. 'Good-bye, Carlo ; God bless and help you!'

'Thank you,' answered the other in a broken voice, realizing what the loss of this friend would be.

'Do always as your sister would wish,' went on Marchese Vanutelli, 'and you will never be in the wrong.'

And as he was leaving the house, a strange mist before his eyes, he met Treherne coming up the road. Very little passed between the two men, who loved each other even then as friends, as though nothing had ever come between them. It was the Marchese who was the quieter of the two, when he saw the other's sorrow.

'We shall meet again,' he said ; 'and absence will not have lessened our friendship.'

'No,' answered Treherne. 'I owe everything to you.'

'That knowledge is my reward,' said Marchese Vanutelli. 'I know in leaving her to you she will be very happy. I promised her mother to see she was so, and now I can leave her.'

And he went away from the old Quaracchi farm, whose white walls were shining in the sunlight between the olive groves and vineyards. He had fulfilled his promise to her mother. Every thought had given way before the one for her happiness.

* * * * *

Treherne entered the house almost in a dream. He went up the stairs mechanically to his accustomed place during Lidia's illness —the studio. On passing her door he saw it was ajar; he could just catch a glimpse of the great arm-chair he had bought for her in Florence. The temptation was too strong; Treherne could not resist it. He pushed open the door and stood in the room. Lidia was seated in the chair he had seen, her head resting back on the pillows. She turned at the noise and saw him. Only a few steps brought him to her.

'Oh, Francesco!' she cried, unable to say any more.

'You are getting better. Why shouldn't I see you?' he asked half defiantly.

Lidia smiled.

'Yes, I am getting better,' she answered, laying her hand on his shoulder, and looking up at him with her clear brown eyes. 'You have been very good,' she faltered; 'there was nothing I wanted that I did not have. Why did you do so much for me?'

'Because I love you,' he answered. 'Oh, Lidia, it is good to see you again getting better!'

'God is good,' she said. She looked wistfully up into his face, as though trying to read his thoughts, her heart beating violently. 'Let us thank God.'

'He is very good and merciful,' replied Treherne in a low voice.

There was a long silence. Lidia clasped her thin white hands over the strong brown hand resting on her knee. She closed her eyes, her lips were faintly moving, and Treherne, looking with reverence and love on her face, knew her thanksgiving was great and speechless. At last she opened her eyes.

'We want for nothing more,' she said simply.

'Only a little more,' corrected Treherne. 'You are not my wife yet.'

'And the picture—you liked the picture?' she asked eagerly.

'It saved me,' he said in a low voice, 'with you and Marchese Vanutelli.'

'Ah!' she said, 'how is Marchese?'

'He is going away from Florence for a little while,' answered Treherne, wondering whether he ought to tell her or not.

'Yes,' she said, evidently thinking he would be away, as he said, 'only for a little while.' 'He is very good, Marchese; and I should like you to be friends with him, Francesco.'

'Yes, my darling,' he answered in a scarcely audible voice.

'Signore, was not this strictly forbidden?' asked the Contessa, endeavouring to look stern as she stood beside them.

Treherne rose, looking rather shamefaced; and Lidia's face showed its first signs of colour since her illness.

'It has done her no harm, I hope?' asked Treherne anxiously.

'No, no,' replied Contessa Mirandoli, altering her severe tone, and looking her merry self. 'I dare say it has done Lidia good. And here is Signorina Trerni. I dare say, if the brother is allowed to make his visit, the sister is too.'

And she drew aside with the gay little laugh no one had heard for a long time now, as Miss Treherne came in and embraced Lidia lovingly.

'We will leave the two together, signore,' said the Contessa. 'Come downstairs with me. I want you,' she added in a low voice, 'to see if you can rouse up Carlo before he sees his sister, for he is very much upset. Poor boy! I suppose there is some good in him, after all.'

'You are quite happy now, are you not?' asked Maisy Treherne a little wistfully when they were left alone.

'There are only a few more things wanting,' said Lidia. 'Oh, signorina, come to us!'

She spoke quickly and eagerly.

'Come to you!' echoed Miss Treherne, smiling a little. 'Why, here I am.'

'Oh, you do not understand,' answered Lidia, as she caressed her friend's hands. 'I want you to come to us. Our Church is so beautiful!'

'Oh, Contessa!' exclaimed the English lady. 'Perhaps—who knows? You are so good! How can anyone help thinking that what you believe in is good and right too? But—but the Madonna. It seems to me you revere and love her more than God.'

'Oh no,' answered Lidia quickly. 'We pray to the Madonna, we love and reverence her, because she is God's Mother. In loving and praying to her we honour God. If she had not been His Mother, if God had not raised her above all His creatures, we should not pray to her as we do. In honouring and loving her we please Almighty God, Who made her beautiful soul.'

'But why should He have made her better than the rest of us?' asked Miss Treherne.

Lidia looked at her friend with wondering eyes.

'Surely,' she said, 'God would not have allowed the Mother of His Son to be sinful like the rest of us? He would create her soul all fair and beautiful, and make her the purest and holiest of His creatures—"*full* of grace."'

Miss Treherne was deeply moved, and for several moments she could not speak. Then she said:

'You are a good little girl, Contessa, and you will pray for me.'

'Oh, so much! so much!' answered Lidia eagerly.

'And I want you to come up and stay at Fiesole with me very soon; the doctor says you can,' went on Miss Treherne. 'You want a change of scene and air, no matter how small it may be. And you will come, dear, won't you?'

'You are very good; I should like it very much,' answered Lidia simply.

'And — and,' hesitated Miss Treherne, thinking she had better make the confession immediately, 'I don't want you to be startled when you get there, Lidia; but your picture—the "Madonnna's Shrine," you know—belongs to us.'

'Belongs to you!' repeated Lidia mechanically.

'Yes, dear,' replied Miss Treherne hastily; 'and you will see it there. Lidia! Lidia! What is it?'

'And I paid you with your own money!' cried Lidia, clasping her hands, and turning white to the very lips. 'Oh, signorina, you told me nothing! Why did you not tell me?'

'My dear child!' exclaimed Miss Treherne, whose brother had never mentioned to her about the money Lidia had paid back, and who had therefore no idea the news would distress her so much.

Then Lidia covered her face with her hands and burst out crying, and Miss Treherne could do nothing to console, till at last she ran to the door and called out for her brother —instinct telling her his comfort would avail better than hers.

He was beside Lidia in a very short time, with his arms round her, endeavouring to calm her grief.

'I am very proud—it is that that makes me mind,' she kept on saying.

'Then it is very foolish of you to upset yourself like this,' he said, trying to be severe.

'You never told me!' she exclaimed. 'What must you have thought?'

'Thought!' echoed Treherne. 'I thought you were the most honourable little girl in all creation to give your first earnings to pay this dreadful debt. My darling, don't cry any more. Just think how it grieves me, you proud little woman!'

'Oh yes, of course,' she said, drying her eyes. 'I will not cry any more.'

And then Carlo came up to see his sister. He was not allowed to stay very long with her, for his grief and remorse distressed her very much. His punishment was great, but the Madonna had heard his sister's prayer, and recalled him to the path of duty, and he was safe.

CONCLUSION.

THE Villa Donati on the Fiesole hill was shining in the glow of sunset; the blue line of the distant Lucchese mountains stood out in strong relief against the golden sky. Below in the valley the town was in shadow, and seemed to be sleeping peacefully, as Treherne with his wife paused to look at the fair scene before entering the house.

They stood together, her hand resting on his arm, and for a long time neither spoke. Then Treherne looked down into the sweet face of his Italian wife, who had brought him back to God.

'My darling, I believe you are a saint!' he exclaimed, drawing her closer to himself.

'No, no,' she answered with a smile, 'far from it. I wish I were. You think that because the Madonna has been so good as to hear my prayer for you and Maisy.'

'And this is the end,' said Treherne, looking over the beautiful valley below, the Arno winding amongst the fertile vineyards and reflecting the golden sky. 'Such a happy end!'

'Oh no, not the end,' replied his wife. 'It is only the beginning. The end will never come; for when we die God will receive us, unworthy as we are, for all eternity.'

And the setting sun shone on the face of the Italian lady, lighting up her earnest dark eyes and firm sweet mouth. It shone beyond her into the drawing-room on two pictures: one of a wayside Crucifix, with the young man pausing to look back on the reverent face of the poor *contadino;* the other is the white stone shrine of the Madonna at Quaracchi.

* * * * *

Marchese Vanutelli was welcomed back to Florence by all his friends some few years after, and of all who were pleased to see him, none were more so than the Signore and Signora Trerni up at the Fiesole villa. It is true a change had taken place, for he was more silent than before; but otherwise there is little difference. And he is very happy now. Merry childish laughter often echoes in the lofty rooms of the old palazzo, and childish figures dance in, always sure of a welcome. And to these children, as to their father and mother, there is only one Marchese.

THE END.

www.ingramcontent.com/pod-product-compliance
Lightning Source LLC
Chambersburg PA
CBHW031736230426
43669CB00007B/368